Developing Numeracy
CALCULATIONS
ACTIVITIES FOR THE DAILY MATHS LESSON

year
2

Peter Patilla

A & C BLACK

Contents

Subtracting two-digit numbers

Multiplying

Dividing

Multiplying and dividing

Resources

Answers

Published 2002 by A & C Black (Publishers) Limited
37 Soho Square, London W1D 3QZ

ISBN 0-7136-6063-5

Copyright text © Peter Patilla, 2002
Copyright illustrations © Kirsty Wilson, 2002
Copyright cover illustration © Charlotte Hard, 2002
Editors: Lynne Williamson and Marie Lister

The author and publishers would like to thank Madeleine Madden and Corinne McCrum for their advice in producing this series of books.

A CIP catalogue record for this book is available from the British Library.

Printed in Great Britain by Caligraving Ltd, Thetford, Norfolk.

Introduction

Developing Numeracy: Calculations is a series of seven photocopiable activity books designed to be used during the daily maths lesson. They focus on the second strand of the National Numeracy Strategy Framework for teaching mathematics. The activities are intended to be used in the time allocated to pupil activities; they aim to reinforce the knowledge, understanding and skills taught during the main part of the lesson and to provide practice and consolidation of the objectives contained in the framework document.

Year 2 supports the teaching of mathematics by providing a series of activities which develop important calculation skills. On the whole the activities are designed for children to work on independently, although this is not always possible and occasionally some children may need support.

Year 2 encourages children to:

- use and extend the vocabulary and understanding of addition, subtraction, multiplication and division;
- know that addition and subtraction are inverse operations and that one 'undoes' the other;
- know that addition can be done in any order but subtraction cannot;
- use the signs +, −, x, ÷ and = ;
- use symbols to stand for unknown numbers;
- total several numbers;
- know by heart all the addition facts for numbers within and including 10;
- start remembering addition and subtraction facts for numbers to at least 20;
- use complementary addition and subtraction facts;
- learn to double and halve a range of numbers and recognise 'near doubles';
- use a range of mental skills to add and subtract two-digit numbers;
- add and subtract near multiples of 10 such as 9, 19, 11, 21;
- use known facts to solve calculations with larger numbers;
- bridge confidently over a multiple of 10 when adding and subtracting a single-digit number;
- add and subtract two-digit numbers without bridging;
- understand multiplication as repeated addition and as describing an array;
- know by heart the 2 and 10 times tables and some, if not all, of the 5 times table;
- understand division as equal sharing and grouping, including remainders;
- know and use halving and doubling, realising that they are inverse operations.

Extension

Many of the activity sheets end with a challenge (**Now try this!**) which reinforces and extends the children's learning, and provides the teacher with the opportunity for assessment. On occasion it may be necessary to read the instructions with the children before they begin the activity. For some of the challenges the children will need to record their answers on a separate piece of paper.

Organisation

Very little equipment is needed, but it will be useful to have available: coloured pencils, counters, scissors and dice. Some children may need number lines and number tracks; these can be found on pages 62 and 63. However, it is important to remember that over-reliance on these resources can become habit-forming. Children should be encouraged to use mental strategies.

Other useful counting equipment includes unit apparatus, such as interlocking cubes, and rod apparatus, such as number rods. To help children understand concepts and develop a wide range of mathematical language, they should have regular opportunities to use both unit and rod apparatus.

The activities in this book will naturally bring in elements of counting and problem solving. Children need to be confident and efficient in counting to be able to develop their calculation skills effectively. They will need regular counting practice to consolidate and develop the skills outlined in the Numbers and the Number System strand of the Strategy for Year 2 (see **Developing Numeracy: Numbers and the Number System Year 2**).

To help teachers select appropriate learning experiences for the children, the activities are grouped into sections within this book. However, the activities are not expected to be used in that order; the sheets are intended to support, rather than direct, the teacher's planning. Some activities are deliberately more challenging than others, to allow for the widely varying ability in most classrooms. Many activities can be made easier or more challenging by masking and substituting some of the numbers. You may wish to re-use some pages by copying them onto card and laminating them, or by enlarging them onto A3 paper.

Teachers' notes

Brief notes are provided at the foot of each page giving ideas and suggestions for maximising the effectiveness of the activity sheets. These can be masked before copying.

Calculation strategies

During Year 2, children are expected to move towards quick recall strategies, knowing the number facts within 10 by heart, and the 2 and 10 times tables. For all other calculations they should be encouraged to use efficient counting strategies and apply known facts. Children should be steered towards using mental strategies rather than relying on counting aids such as counters or number lines. To develop mental strategies, the role of sophisticated counting skills is crucial. These counting skills include:

- counting on and back from a range of numbers;
- counting on and back by a stated amount;
- counting on and back between a pair of numbers, keeping tally of how many;
- counting on and back in units other than 1, such as 2, 5 and 10;
- knowing 1 and 10 more/less than another number without counting;
- comfortably bridging multiples of 10 and 100 when counting on and back.

Note on multiplication: Common practice is to describe the × sign as 'lots of' or 'groups of' (which younger children find easier to understand), rather than the more precise 'multiplied by'. This 'lots of' approach has the effect of reversing the repeated addition: for example, 3 multiplied by 4 (3 + 3 + 3 + 3) becomes 3 lots of 4 (4 + 4 + 4). What is critical in the teaching of multiplication is the fact that the order of multiplication does not matter, i.e. $3 \times 4 = 4 \times 3$. If this is done it matters less which convention is taught.

A school needs to decide whether to initially teach multiplication using 'lots of' to describe the × sign or the slightly more mathematical 'multiplied by'.

Throughout this series, multiplication is treated as 'lots of' for continuity.

Whole-class warm-up activities

The following activities provide some practical ideas which can be used to introduce the main teaching part of the lesson.

Unison response

Ask a mental calculation question to which you want a fairly rapid response. Clap your hands three times, then open your hands. The claps allow for thinking time. The children should respond in unison when you open your hands. Over a period of time, gradually reduce the time between claps to decrease the thinking time.

Show me

Provide each child with a set of number cards, which they should arrange face up in front of them for quick and easy access. Say a calculation to be solved mentally. On hearing the command 'Show me', the children hold up the cards showing the answer. Over the course of the year, gradually decrease the thinking time.

What is the question?

Write a number on the board, such as 12, and explain that this is the answer to a calculation. Ask a child to come to the board and write any calculation which has the answer 12, for example 10 + 2. Draw a large box around the calculation. Ask other children to write more calculations with the answer 12. If a calculation is the same type as the one in the box (in this example an addition), it should be written in the box. Otherwise it should go in another box. In this way the pupils' responses are sorted into types of calculation.

Cover up

Give each child a number grid or track (see pages 62 and 63), and several counters or cubes. Ask the children to solve a calculation and cover the answer on the grid, for example: Cover the total of 13 and 7. You could also ask questions which have a range of possible answers, for example: Cover two numbers that have a difference of 9; Cover two numbers that total 100. Discuss the various answers given by the children.

Silent response

Ask the children to sit with their eyes closed and their hands stretched out in front of them. Give a range of statements, some true and some untrue, for example: The total of 13 and 5 is odd. The product of 4 and 3 is even. If the statement is true, the children should raise their hands in the air. If it is untrue, they should put their hands on their knees. You could clap your hands a short time after making the statement, to signal the moment when the children should respond.

Fairground fun 1

- ## Do these as quickly as you can.

$4 + 6 = \boxed{10}$ $3 + 5 = \square$ $7 + 1 = \square$

$10 - 5 = \square$ $7 - 4 = \square$ $8 - 3 = \square$

$4 + 3 = \square$ $9 - 5 = \square$ $8 + 2 = \square$

$10 - 0 = \square$ $6 + 2 = \square$ $5 - 3 = \square$

- ## Write the answers.

BOUNCY CASTLE

7 plus 2 equals $\square$ 8 subtract 4 leaves $\square$

Double 4 is $\square$ 2 added to 6 makes $\square$

4 less than 9 is $\square$ 9 minus 6 equals $\square$

Now try this!

- ## Use $\boxed{\text{odd}}$ numbers to write three additions and three subtractions.

Are the answers **odd** or **even**?

Teachers' note The children should work on knowing all the number bonds to 10 by heart. Encourage them to use mental strategies rather than relying on counting aids. You could give them flashcards which have a calculation on one side and the answer on the back. The children can work in pairs to test each other, answering quickly.

Developing Numeracy Calculations Year 2 © A & C Black 2002

Fairground fun 2

• **Write the missing numbers.**

$3 + 2 = \boxed{5}$ ★

$4 + 3 = $ ★

$1 + 5 = $ ★

$9 - 1 = $ ★

$6 - 4 = $ ★

$5 - 5 = $ ★

$5 + $ ★ $ = 8$

$6 - $ ★ $ = 2$

$9 - $ ★ $ = 6$

★ $ - 3 = 7$

$7 + 2 = $ ★

$10 - 2 = $ ★

★ $ - 1 = 0$

$0 + $ ★ $ = 4$

• **Write three** | calculations | **for each number.**

6

3

9

```
10 - 4
3 + 3
10 - 7 + 3
```

Teachers' note Talk about the strategies that the children use to solve the missing number problems. In the extension, introduce the word 'calculations'.

Developing Numeracy
Calculations Year 2
© A & C Black 2002

7

Alien machines

• **Write the missing numbers.**

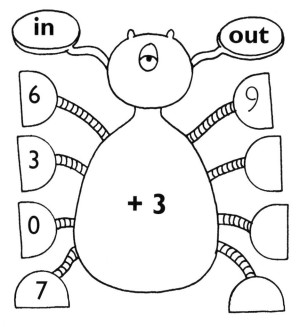

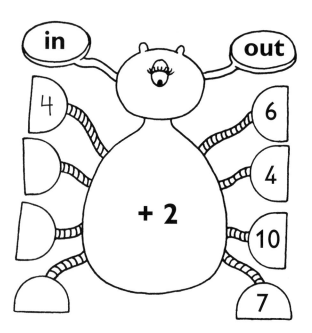

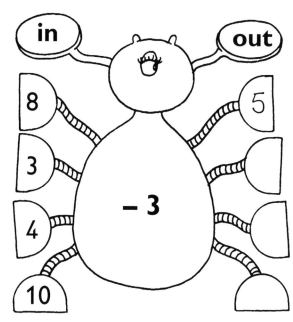

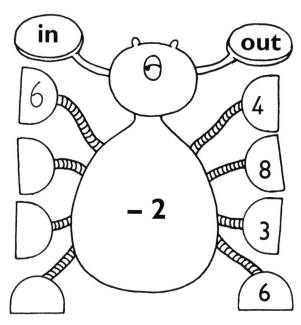

• Draw a ⊞ + 4 machine and a ⊟ − 5 machine.

• Write ⎡in⎤ numbers on the ⊞ + 4 machine.

• Write ⎡out⎤ numbers on the ⊟ − 5 machine.

• Give them to a partner to solve.

Teachers' note Talk about an addition 'undoing' a subtraction, and vice versa, before the children begin the activity.

Developing Numeracy
Calculations Year 2
© A & C Black 2002

Gone fishing

- **Write the answers.**
- **Join the fish to the boat with the same answer.**

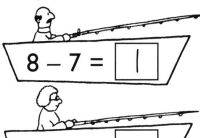

$8 - 7 = \boxed{1}$

$10 - 7 = \boxed{}$

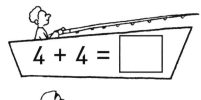

$4 + 4 = \boxed{}$

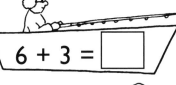

$6 + 3 = \boxed{}$

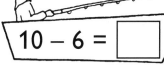

$10 - 6 = \boxed{}$

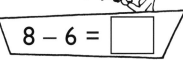

$8 - 6 = \boxed{}$

$7 + 3 = \boxed{}$

$9 - 3 = \boxed{}$

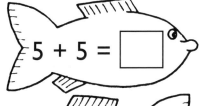

$5 + 5 = \boxed{}$

$8 - 5 = \boxed{}$

$6 - 4 = \boxed{}$

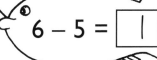

$6 - 5 = \boxed{1}$

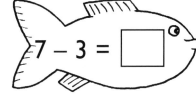

$7 - 3 = \boxed{}$

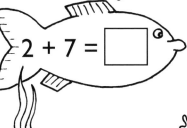

$2 + 7 = \boxed{}$

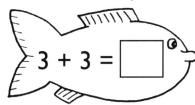

$3 + 3 = \boxed{}$

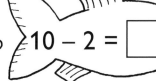

$10 - 2 = \boxed{}$

- **Write three more calculations with the answer $\boxed{12}$.**

$15 - 3 = 12$

Teachers' note The children should start by recording each answer. Encourage them to do the calculations quickly. They could use different-coloured pencils for the joining lines.

Developing Numeracy
Calculations Year 2
© A & C Black 2002

Wordsearch fun

- ## Find these words in the grid. Ring them.

| ~~add~~ | ~~less~~ | subtract | more | equals | total |

n	s	a	d	d	o	t	o	t	a	l	l	l
m	o	r	e	u	x	p	b	v	l	c	e
u	b	e	q	u	a	l	s	p	t	p	s
s	u	b	t	r	a	c	t	o	x	k	s

- ## Write the answers. Ring the number words.

9 + 3 = [12]   5 + 4 = [ ]   9 − 2 = [ ]

3 + 3 = [ ]   6 − 4 = [ ]   3 + 2 = [ ]

10 − 6 = [ ]   2 + 8 = [ ]   8 − 5 = [ ]

6 − 5 = [ ]   7 + 1 = [ ]

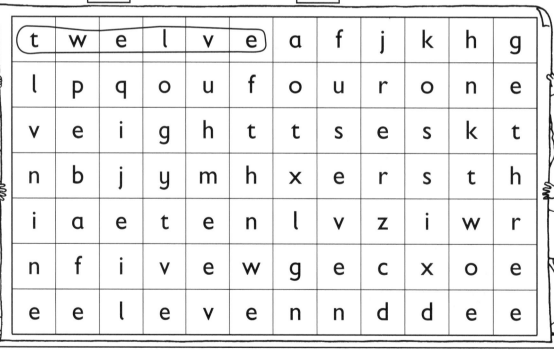

t	w	e	l	v	e	a	f	j	k	h	g
l	p	q	o	u	f	o	u	r	o	n	e
v	e	i	g	h	t	t	s	e	s	k	t
n	b	j	y	m	h	x	e	r	s	t	h
i	a	e	t	e	n	l	v	z	i	w	r
n	f	i	v	e	w	g	e	c	x	o	e
e	e	l	e	v	e	n	n	d	d	e	e

- ## Find another number word in the second wordsearch. _____

Teachers' note Check that the children know how to use a wordsearch. They could work in small groups to support each other. Some may need a word-bank to refer to. As a further extension, the children could write number sentences which include the maths words they have found.

**Developing Numeracy
Calculations Year 2
© A & C Black 2002**

Rabbit addition

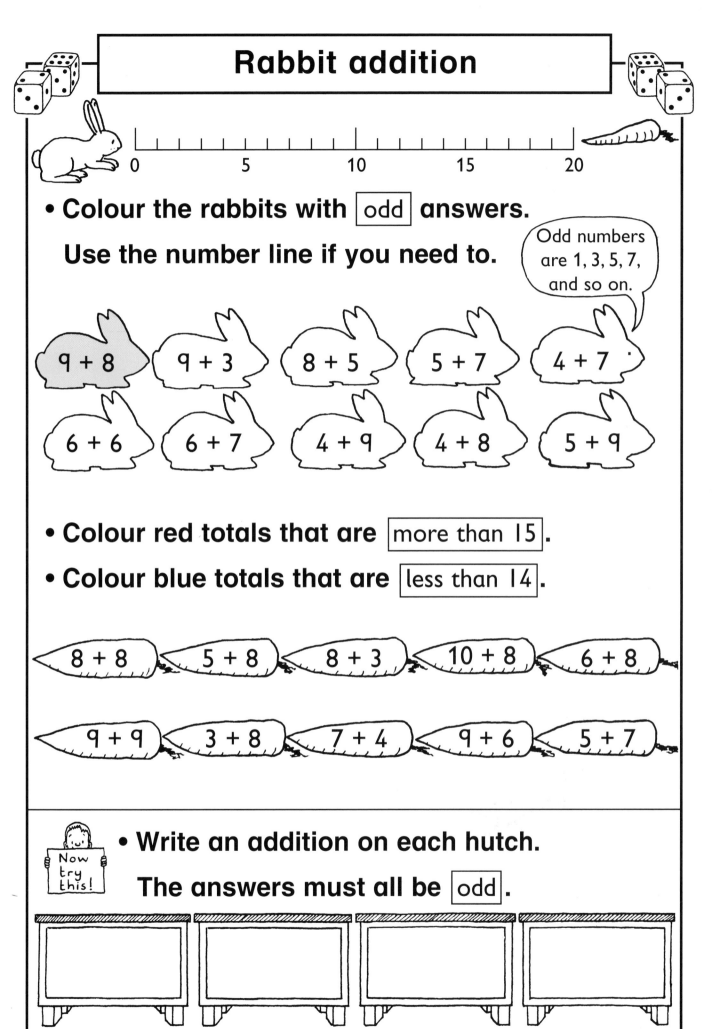

0   5   10   15   20

• **Colour the rabbits with** boxed(odd) **answers.**

Use the number line if you need to.

Odd numbers are 1, 3, 5, 7, and so on.

9 + 8   9 + 3   8 + 5   5 + 7   4 + 7

6 + 6   6 + 7   4 + 9   4 + 8   5 + 9

• **Colour red totals that are** more than 15.
• **Colour blue totals that are** less than 14.

8 + 8   5 + 8   8 + 3   10 + 8   6 + 8

9 + 9   3 + 8   7 + 4   9 + 6   5 + 7

Now try this!

• **Write an addition on each hutch.**

The answers must all be odd.

Teachers' note Check that the children know that the order of adding does not matter. Discuss the results of adding odd and even numbers. In the second activity, ensure the children realise that 15 is not included in the set of numbers which are 'more than 15'. Similarly 14 is not in the set 'less than 14'. These carrots should be left blank.

**Developing Numeracy
Calculations Year 2
© A & C Black 2002**

Lorry addition

• **Write the missing numbers on each lorry.**

$12 + 5 =$ ☐ $7 + 11 =$ ☐

$11 + 4 =$ ☐ $4 + 12 =$ ☐

$15 + 3 =$ ☐ $5 + 15 =$ ☐

$14 + 6 =$ ☐ $8 + 11 =$ ☐

$10 = 10 +$ $\boxed{0}$ $13 =$ ☐ $+ 3$

$12 = 10 +$ ☐ $11 =$ ☐ $+ 1$

$14 = 10 +$ ☐ $17 =$ ☐ $+ 7$

$16 = 10 +$ ☐ $19 =$ ☐ $+ 9$

 The three corner numbers total $\boxed{15}$.

• **Write the missing numbers.**

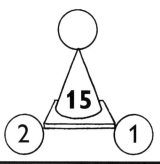
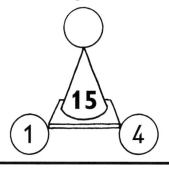
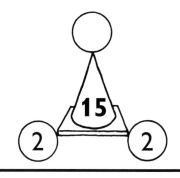

Teachers' note Check that the children understand the tens and ones structure for numbers between 9 and 20. Talk about the strategies used to answer the problems, such as adding on from the larger number and 'remembering'.

**Developing Numeracy
Calculations Year 2
© A & C Black 2002**

Making 20

- ## Make each card total 20 .

4 + 16

7 + ▢

▢ + 18

▢ + 2

▢ + 9

14 + ▢

- ## Join number pairs to total 20 .

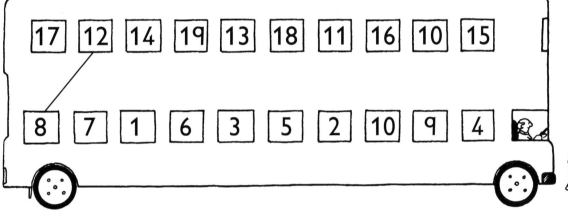

| 17 | 12 | 14 | 19 | 13 | 18 | 11 | 16 | 10 | 15 |

| 8 | 7 | 1 | 6 | 3 | 5 | 2 | 10 | 9 | 4 |

- ## Write the missing numbers.

20 = ▢ + 0   20 = 7 + ▢

20 = ▢ + 4   20 = 6 + ▢

20 = ▢ + 1   20 = 5 + ▢

20 = ▢ + 3   20 = 9 + ▢

20 = ▢ + 2   20 = 8 + ▢

Teachers' note It is important that children have plenty of practice in recognising pairs of numbers that total 20. As an oral starter activity, give the children a number such as 12, and ask what must be added to make 20. Encourage them to use known facts, for example, 2 + 8 = 10 can help them work out that 12 + 8 = 20.

**Developing Numeracy
Calculations Year 2
© A & C Black 2002**

13

• **Follow the instructions to help you find the mystery words.**

☆ Write the missing number in each calculation.

☆ Go round the wheel to find these numbers in order.

☆ Write the first letter of each picture as you come to it.

The words are _S_ _ _ _ _ _ **and** _ _ _ _ _ _ _ .

5 + [7] = 12

6 + 8 = [ ]

[ ] + 15 = 18

0 + [ ] = 17

[ ] + 14 = 19

6 + [ ] = 12

[ ] + 7 = 20

8 + [ ] = 16

[ ] + 5 = 14

9 + [ ] = 13

12 + 8 = [ ]

9 + [ ] = 11

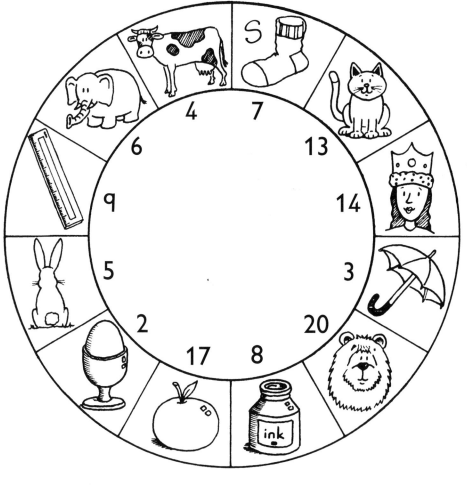

Teachers' note Check that the children understand the instructions and discuss strategies for finding the missing numbers. The children should write the matching letters to the calculations one by one as they are answered, or tick off the completed calculations in order as they write the letters.

**Developing Numeracy
Calculations Year 2
© A & C Black 2002**

Rabbit subtraction

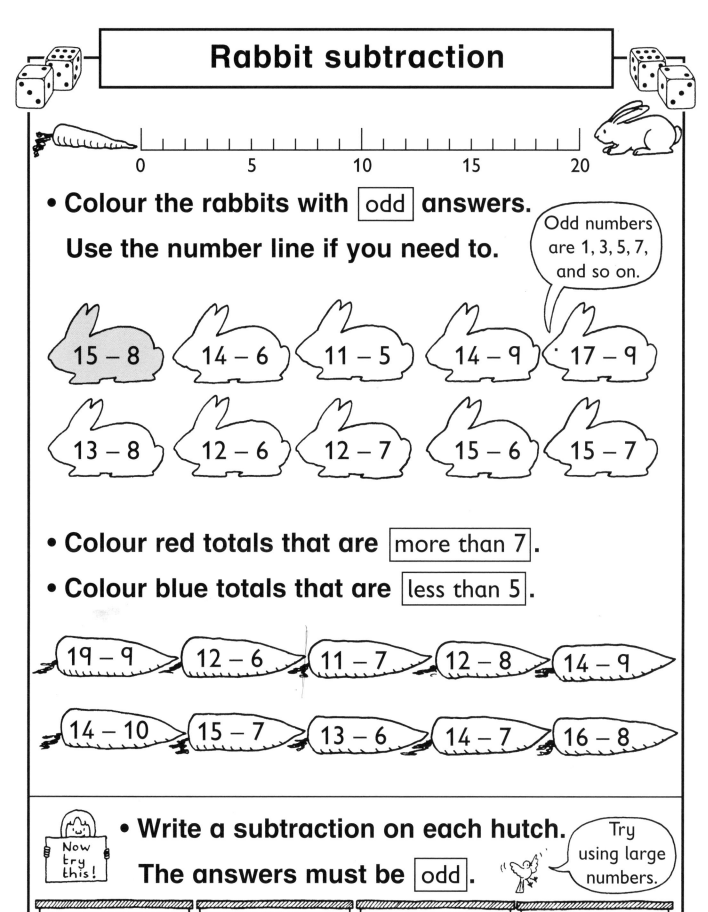

0   5   10   15   20

- **Colour the rabbits with** | odd | **answers.**

  Use the number line if you need to.

  Odd numbers are 1, 3, 5, 7, and so on.

  15 – 8   14 – 6   11 – 5   14 – 9   17 – 9

  13 – 8   12 – 6   12 – 7   15 – 6   15 – 7

- **Colour red totals that are** | more than 7 |**.**
- **Colour blue totals that are** | less than 5 |**.**

  19 – 9   12 – 6   11 – 7   12 – 8   14 – 9

  14 – 10   15 – 7   13 – 6   14 – 7   16 – 8

- **Write a subtraction on each hutch.**

  Now try this!

  The answers must be | odd |**.**

  Try using large numbers.

Teachers' note Discuss the results of subtracting odd and even numbers. Encourage the children to check each subtraction by addition. In the second activity, ensure the children realise that 7 is not included in the set of numbers that are 'more than 7'. Similarly 5 is not in the set 'less than 5'. Carrots which do not fall into either set should be left blank.

**Developing Numeracy
Calculations Year 2
© A & C Black 2002**

Lorry subtraction

Number line: 0 5 10 15 20

• **Write the missing numbers on each lorry.**

Use the number line if you need to.

$17 - 2 = \boxed{}$ $15 - \boxed{} = 13$

$16 - 3 = \boxed{}$ $16 - \boxed{} = 11$

$19 - 7 = \boxed{}$ $20 - \boxed{} = 14$

$10 - 3 = \boxed{}$ $19 - \boxed{} = 15$

$12 = 12 - \boxed{0}$ $13 = \boxed{} - 3$

$12 = 17 - \boxed{}$ $11 = \boxed{} - 1$

$14 = 16 - \boxed{}$ $12 = \boxed{} - 7$

$11 = 18 - \boxed{}$ $15 = \boxed{} - 4$

• **Write four different subtractions.**

$\boxed{} - \boxed{} = 5$ $\boxed{} - \boxed{} = 5$

$\boxed{} - \boxed{} = 5$ $\boxed{} - \boxed{} = 5$

Teachers' note Talk about the strategies that the children use to work out the missing numbers. Putting the answers first helps the children to work on problems such as: 'The answer is 14, what is the question?' In the plenary session, discuss alternative calculations that have a 'teen' answer.

**Developing Numeracy
Calculations Year 2**
© A & C Black 2002

Caterpillar count

• **Write the** difference **between the rows.**

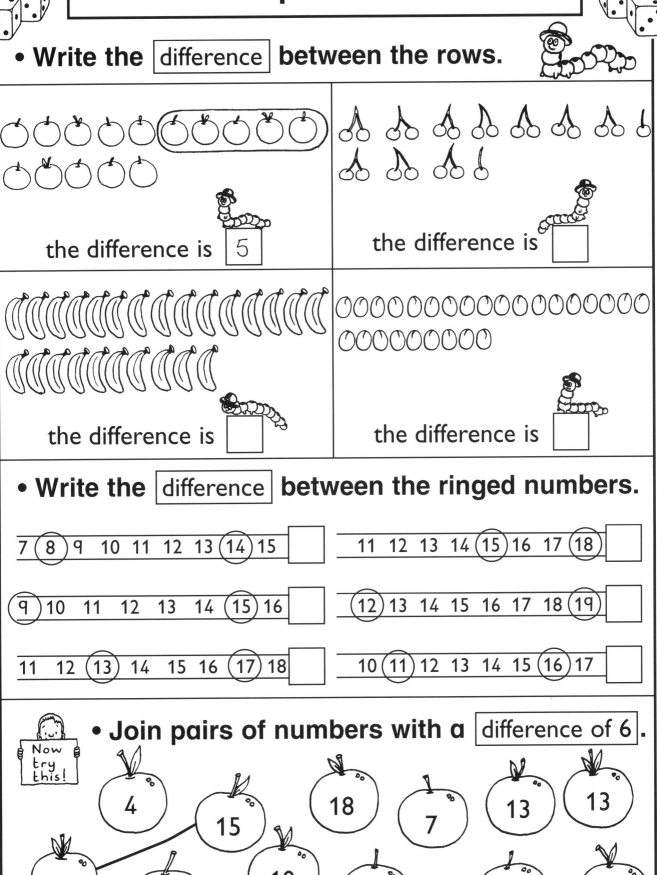

the difference is 5

the difference is ☐

the difference is ☐

the difference is ☐

• **Write the** difference **between the ringed numbers.**

7 ⑧ 9 10 11 12 13 ⑭ 15 ☐

11 12 13 14 ⑮ 16 17 ⑱ ☐

⑨ 10 11 12 13 14 ⑮ 16 ☐

⑫ 13 14 15 16 17 18 ⑲ ☐

11 12 ⑬ 14 15 16 ⑰ 18 ☐

10 ⑪ 12 13 14 15 ⑯ 17 ☐

• **Join pairs of numbers with a** difference of 6 **.**

Now try this!

4   15   18   7   13   13

9   12   10   20   14   19

Teachers' note Revise difference, and explain that it can be found by counting on from the smaller number or by counting back from the larger. It can help to talk about 'number difference' to distinguish it from other differences such as shape, size and colour.

Developing Numeracy
Calculations Year 2
© A & C Black 2002

Where's Mum?

• **Join each duck to its duckling.**

1   2   3   4   5   6   7   8   9

20 – 17   17 – 11   20 – 11

18 – 17   16 – 12   15 – 3

10

11

20 – 0   19 – 2   20 – 10

12

13

20 – 2   20 – 4   17 – 3

14

20   19   18   17   16   15

• **Write the answers. Colour the** | odd one out |.

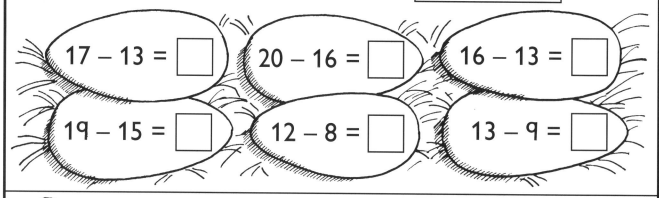

$17 - 13 = \square$ $20 - 16 = \square$ $16 - 13 = \square$

$19 - 15 = \square$ $12 - 8 = \square$ $13 - 9 = \square$

 • **Write six subtractions which all have the same answer.**

Now try this!

Teachers' note Discuss the fact that some subtractions within 20 result in a single-digit answer and some a two-digit answer. As a further extension, the children could write their own subtractions for the ducklings without mums.

**Developing Numeracy
Calculations Year 2**
© A & C Black 2002

Frogs on logs

- **Join each frog to its log.**

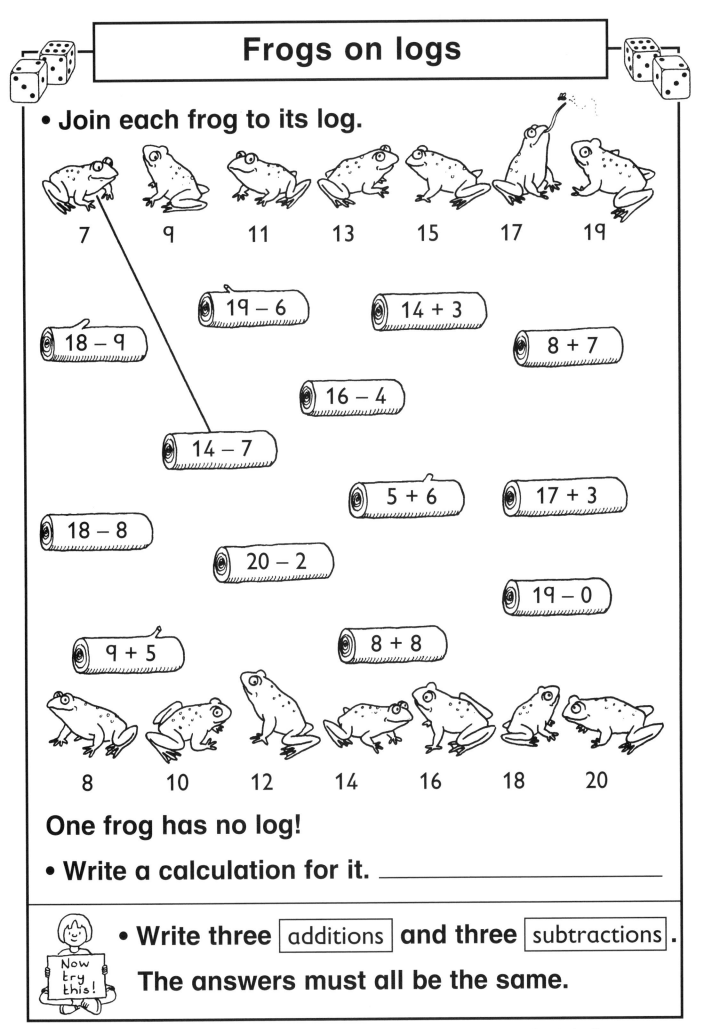

7   9   11   13   15   17   19

18 – 9

19 – 6

14 + 3

8 + 7

16 – 4

14 – 7

18 – 8

5 + 6

17 + 3

20 – 2

19 – 0

9 + 5

8 + 8

8   10   12   14   16   18   20

One frog has no log!

- **Write a calculation for it.** _____

- **Write three** additions **and three** subtractions.
  The answers must all be the same.

Teachers' note Check the strategies that children use to answer each calculation. Some children may need a number line to help them. However, care should be taken to ensure that they do not rely too heavily on number lines, as this can inhibit mental and quick recall strategies.

Developing Numeracy
Calculations Year 2
© A & C Black 2002

Hopping mad!

- **Complete the calculations for each number line.**

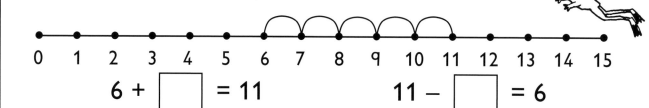

0 1 2 3 4 5 6 7 8 9 10 11 12 13 14 15

$6 + \boxed{} = 11$ $11 - \boxed{} = 6$

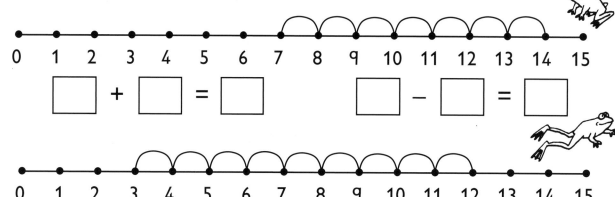

0 1 2 3 4 5 6 7 8 9 10 11 12 13 14 15

$\boxed{} + \boxed{} = \boxed{}$ $\boxed{} - \boxed{} = \boxed{}$

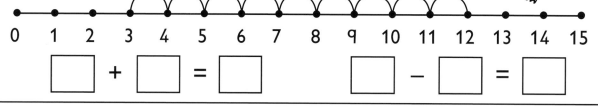

0 1 2 3 4 5 6 7 8 9 10 11 12 13 14 15

$\boxed{} + \boxed{} = \boxed{}$ $\boxed{} - \boxed{} = \boxed{}$

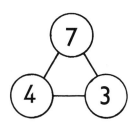

$3 + 4 = 7$
$4 + 3 = 7$
$7 - 3 = 4$
$7 - 4 = 3$

Can you see how 3, 4 and 7 are linked?

- **Write addition and subtraction facts for these.**

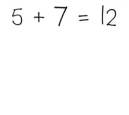 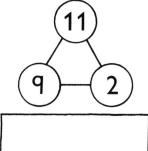 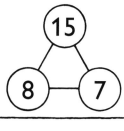

$5 + 7 = 12$

Teachers' note Check that the children can link complementary addition facts with the subtraction facts. Discuss the fact that addition can be done in any order but subtraction cannot (for example, $2 + 7 = 7 + 2$, but it is not true that $7 - 2 = 2 - 7$).

**Developing Numeracy
Calculations Year 2**
© A & C Black 2002

20

Number jigsaw

This is a jigsaw for the numbers $\boxed{1}$ to $\boxed{20}$.

Three pieces are missing.

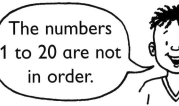

The numbers 1 to 20 are not in order.

- **Work out the calculations to find the missing numbers.**

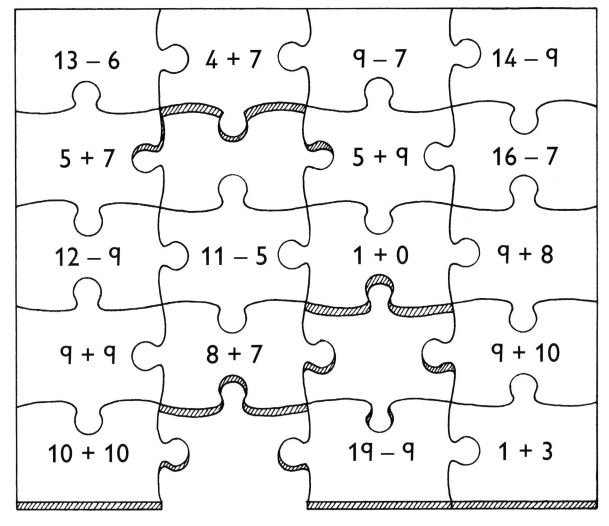

13 − 6	4 + 7	9 − 7	14 − 9
5 + 7		5 + 9	16 − 7
12 − 9	11 − 5	1 + 0	9 + 8
9 + 9	8 + 7		9 + 10
10 + 10		19 − 9	1 + 3

- **Write a calculation on each piece to complete the jigsaw.**

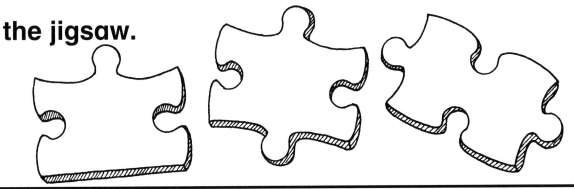

Teachers' note Suggest that the children write the answers to each calculation in the bottom right-hand corner of each jigsaw piece. Check children realise that there are lots of possible additions or subtractions to match the missing pieces in the jigsaw. You could photocopy the page, then mask all the calculations before recopying so that children can create their own number jigsaw puzzle.

Developing Numeracy
Calculations Year 2
© A & C Black 2002

Puzzle squares

• Fill in the missing numbers.

+	4	7	9
6	10		
5			
8			

+		6	
4	9		
7			15
9			

+	7		9
			13
8		11	
		12	

The answers must be correct in **rows** <u>and</u> **columns**.

4	+		=	12
+	■	+	■	+
	+		=	7
=	■	=	■	=
10	+		=	

Rows go across. **Columns** go up and down.

• Fill in the gaps.

Now try this!

8	+		+	1	=	11
−	■	+	■	+	■	−
	+	3	−		=	8
+	■	+	■	+	■	+
4	+	2	−	2	=	
=	■	=	■	=	■	=
5	+		−	5	=	7

Teachers' note Ensure that the children understand how to complete each type of grid. Encourage them to check their results carefully after completing the grids.

**Developing Numeracy
Calculations Year 2
© A & C Black 2002**

Making number sentences

- **Cut out the cards.**

Record each number sentence.

- **Make different number sentences.**

0	1	2	3	4	5	6	7
8	9	10	11	12	13	14	15
16	17	18	19	20	+	−	=

add	plus	more than	altogether

the same as	the total of	subtract

makes	totals	take away	less than

minus	take	from	leaves	equals

is	the difference between	and

Use 8 , 4 and 12 .   Use 16 , 4 and 20 .

Use 9 , 2 and 11 .   Use 12 , 5 and 17 .

Teachers' note Ask the children to choose one of the bottom four cards and work together to make different sentences for the same set of three numbers. Some children could choose their own set of three linked numbers and make different number sentences. Two sets of 0–9 will be needed if they want to use doubles.

**Developing Numeracy
Calculations Year 2
© A & C Black 2002**

Stepping stones

• **Complete the number sequences.**

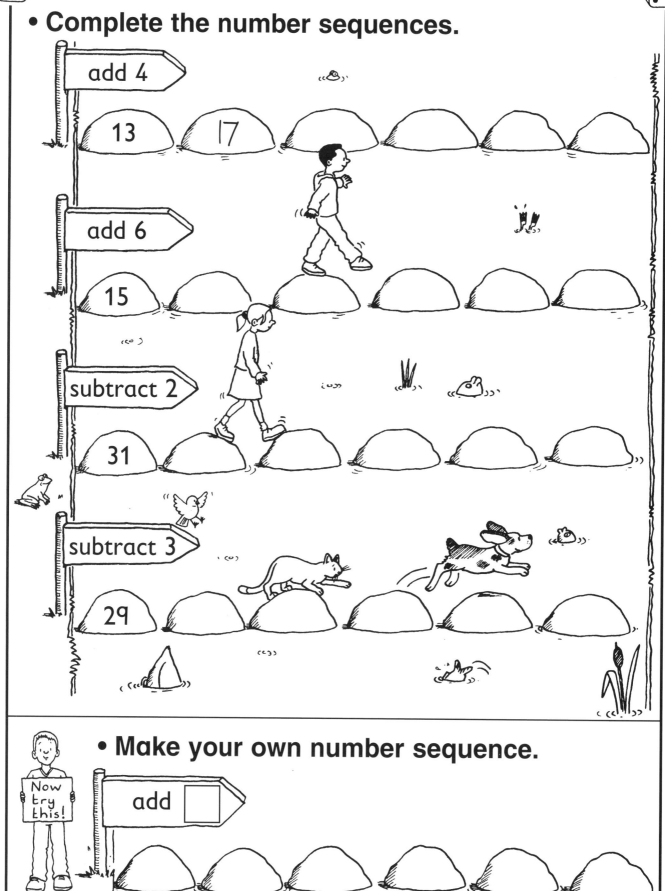

add 4

13   17

add 6

15

subtract 2

31

subtract 3

29

• **Make your own number sequence.**

Now try this!

add ☐

Teachers' note Some children may need to use a number grid or number track (see pages 62 and 63). However, encourage them to use counting skills rather than relying completely on tracks and grids.

**Developing Numeracy
Calculations Year 2
© A & C Black 2002**

Dodgems

- **Write the answers on the cars.**

- **Look for a** pattern **in each row.**

Number patterns can help with addition and subtraction facts.

1. 6 + 3 = 9   16 + 3 = ☐   26 + 3 = ☐

2. 15 + 2 = ☐   25 + 2 = ☐   35 + 2 = ☐

3. 18 − 6 = ☐   28 − 6 = ☐   38 − 6 = ☐

4. 19 − 2 = ☐   29 − 2 = ☐   39 − 2 = ☐

5. 18 + 2 = ☐   28 + 2 = ☐   38 + 2 = ☐

- **Write the next three calculations for each row.**

Look at the pattern.

Example:

1. 36 + 3 = 39   46 + 3 = 49   56 + 3 = 59

Teachers' note Children need plenty of practice in looking for patterns in similar calculations. Encourage them to use a number grid to find the patterns (see page 62).

**Developing Numeracy
Calculations Year 2
© A & C Black 2002**

Fish 'n' chips

• **What must you add to each number to reach the next** | tens number |**?**

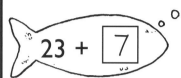
23 + 7 = 30

23 + [7]　　42 + [ ]　　75 + [ ]

51 + [ ]　　72 + [ ]　　58 + [ ]

86 + [ ]　　67 + [ ]　　94 + [ ]

• **Write the missing numbers.**

Take care with the last row!

72 + [ ] = 80　　55 + [ ] = 60　　38 + [ ] = 40

67 + [ ] = 70　　49 + [ ] = 50　　93 + [ ] = 100

4 + [ ] = 50　　2 + [ ] = 70　　8 + [ ] = 100

Now try this!

• **Make each <u>pair</u> of fish total** | 100 |**.**

Example:

55 + [5]　　35 + [5]

71 + [ ]　　16 + [ ]　　42 + [ ]　　48 + [ ]

Teachers' note Practise complements to the 'next ten' with the class using the 'Unison response' activity on page 5. Say a non-tens number and ask the children to say the number that must be added to reach the next ten. Encourage them to use known facts, for example, 3 + 7 = 10 can help them work out that 23 + 7 = 30. A number grid can help to reinforce this (see page 62).

Developing Numeracy Calculations Year 2 © A & C Black 2002

Cheese and biscuits

• **Write the totals.**

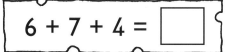

> It doesn't matter in which order you add the numbers.

> Look for pairs that total **10** or **20**.

6 + 7 + 4 = ☐

17 + 5 + 3 = ☐

8 + 12 + 9 = ☐

3 + 17 + 7 = ☐

• **Write the missing numbers.**

1 + 29 + ☐ = 35

7 + 23 + ☐ = 34

5 + 25 + ☐ = 34

37 + 3 + ☐ = 46

39 + ☐ + 9 = 49

35 + ☐ + 3 = 43

9 + ☐ + 2 = 52

5 + ☐ + 8 = 58

Now try this!

• **Write numbers on the mice to total the number on the cheese.**

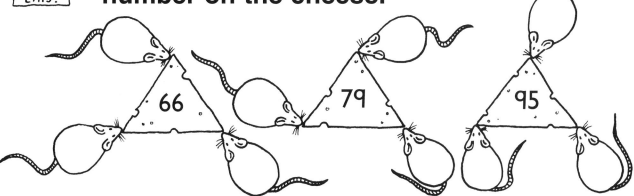

66   79   95

Teachers' note Practise complements to the 'next ten' with the class using the 'Unison response' activity on page 5. Say a non-tens number and ask the children to say the number that must be added to reach the next ten. Encourage them to use known facts, for example, 3 + 7 = 10 can help them work out that 23 + 7 = 30. A number grid can help to reinforce this (see page 62).

Developing Numeracy Calculations Year 2 © A & C Black 2002

Treetop trail

- **Answer the clues. Then follow the number trail to find the animal!**

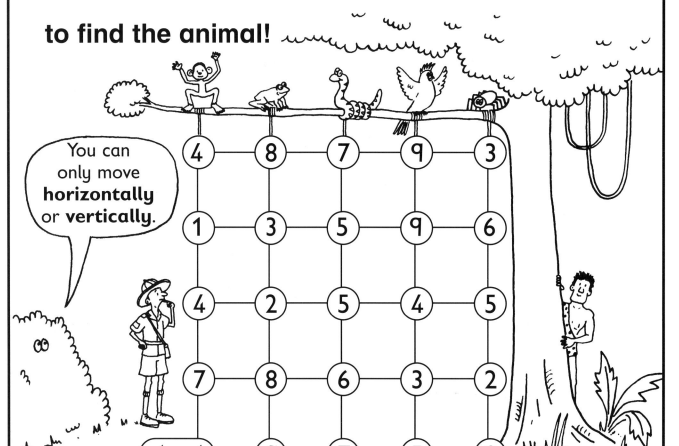

You can only move **horizontally** or **vertically**.

4	8	7	9	3
1	3	5	9	6
4	2	5	4	5
7	8	6	3	2
start	9	7	5	8

Clues

1. 40 + ☐ = 49   **2.** 70 + ☐ = 78   **3.** 80 + ☐ = 82

4. 60 − ☐ = 55   **5.** 80 − ☐ = 76   **6.** 100 − ☐ = 91

7. 90 − ☐ = 85   **8.** 50 − ☐ = 47   **9.** 40 − ☐ = 32

- **The trail leads to the _____ .**

- **Write clues which lead to another animal.**

Teachers' note Children should be comfortable with adding and subtracting a single digit to and from a multiple of 10. Ensure they understand that they should only move across or up the grid (not diagonally). For the extension, the children should work in small groups, co-operating and checking each other's attempts. Encourage them to use larger numbers such as 500 + ☐ = 504.

**Developing Numeracy
Calculations Year 2
© A & C Black 2002**

Balloons

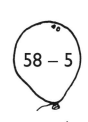

• **Join each balloon to its position on the line.**

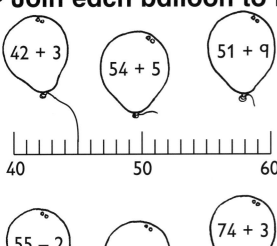

42 + 3   54 + 5   51 + 9   47 − 2   49 − 8   58 − 5

```
40          50          60        40          50          60
```

55 − 2   63 + 5   74 + 3   78 − 7   86 + 3   99 − 5

```
50      60      70      80      90      100
```

• **Write the missing numbers.**

51 + [3]   69 − [ ]   81 + [ ]   98 − [ ]

```
50      60      70      80      90      100
```

• **Write a calculation on each balloon.**

Now try this!

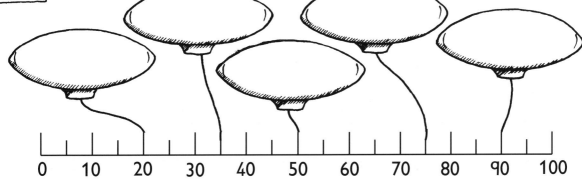

```
0   10   20   30   40   50   60   70   80   90   100
```

Teachers' note Children should be comfortable with adding and subtracting a single digit to and from a two-digit number where no bridging is involved. In the extension, they may include bridging if they are able.

**Developing Numeracy
Calculations Year 2
© A & C Black 2002**

Elephant ears

• **Write the missing numbers.**

Both ears must have the same answer.

30 + 40   20 + | 50 | 50 + 20   10 + | |

20 + | | 30 + 30   30 + | | 80 + 20

60 + 40   10 + | | 400 + 300   100 + | |

200 + 400   100 + | | 300 + 300   400 + | |

300 + 600   200 + | | 500 + 300   600 + | |

• **Write your own additions.**

Both ears must have the same answer.

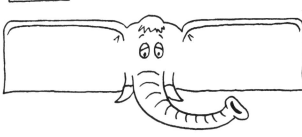
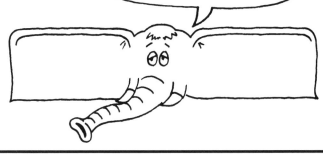

Teachers' note Children should be comfortable with adding multiples of 10 and 100. Encourage them to use known facts, for example, 3 + 4 = 7 can help them work out that 30 + 40 = 70. For the extension, you can either restrict the numbers to be used (for example, multiples of 10 or multiples of 100), or leave it open.

**Developing Numeracy
Calculations Year 2
© A & C Black 2002**

Monster cards

• **Play this game with a partner.**

☆ Cut out the cards. Spread them face down.

☆ Take turns to pick a card. Say what number must be added to make 100 .

☆ If your partner agrees, keep the card. If not, put it back.

☆ The winner is the player with the most cards at the end.

Teachers' note Complements to 100 are important, especially knowing addition pairs which are multiples of 10. Encourage the children to do the calculations mentally. They should decide together whether the answer is correct, using calculation aids if necessary. They could use a number grid or number track for non-multiples of 10 (see pages 62 and 63).

Developing Numeracy Calculations Year 2 © A & C Black 2002

• **Solve this puzzle.**

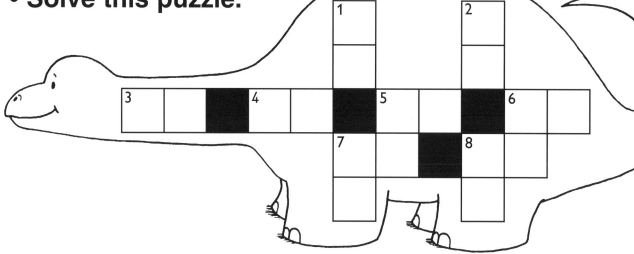

Across	Down
3. 20 + 37	**1.** 43 + 40
4. 10 + 23	**2.** 57 + 20
5. 30 + 56	**5.** 51 + 30
6. 40 + 28	**6.** 14 + 50
7. 50 + 11	**7.** 32 + 30
8. 30 + 64	**8.** 55 + 40

Each egg is the total of the two underneath it.

• **Fill in the missing numbers.**

• **Make your own egg puzzles.**

• **Give them to a partner to solve.**

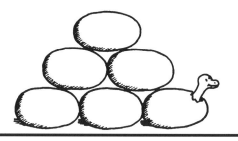

Teachers' note These puzzles involve adding a multiple of 10 to a two-digit number. If necessary, the children could use a number grid or number track (see pages 62 and 63). However, encourage mental strategies wherever possible.

**Developing Numeracy
Calculations Year 2
© A & C Black 2002**

Frog hops

• **Write the missing numbers.**

43 + ⬡ = 73   72 + ⬡ = 92   18 + ⬡ = 18

55 + ⬡ = 65   11 + ⬡ = 61   44 + ⬡ = 84

40 + ⬡ = 56   10 + ⬡ = 77   30 + ⬡ = 44

60 + ⬡ = 75   80 + ⬡ = 93   10 + ⬡ = 87

20 more than  equals 75.

The total of 50 and 🐸 is 88.

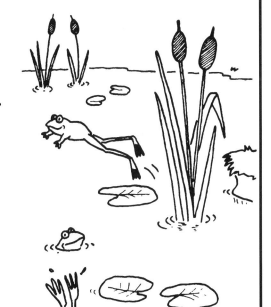

70 plus 🐸 equals 83.

🐸 added to 62 equals 82.

The sum of 20 and 🐸 is 67.

• **Write your own calculations on the lilypads.**

⬡ + ⬡ = 58   ⬡ + ⬡ = 61

⬡ + ⬡ = 73   ⬡ + ⬡ = 84

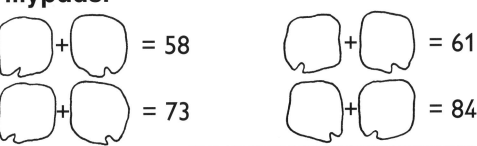

Teachers' note This activity involves adding a multiple of 10 to a two-digit number. If necessary, the children could use a number grid or number track (see pages 62 and 63). However, encourage mental strategies wherever possible.

Developing Numeracy Calculations Year 2 © A & C Black 2002

Snack stop!

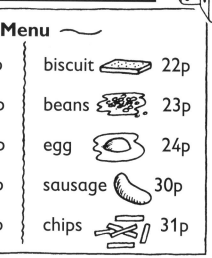

• Write the cost.

~ Menu ~

cola	11p	biscuit		22p
juice	15p	beans		23p
cake	18p	egg		24p
toast	20p	sausage		30p
bun	21p	chips		31p

1. __21__ p + __11__ p

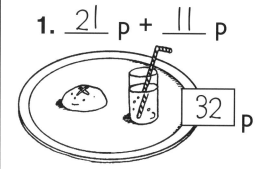

32 p

2. ___ p + ___ p

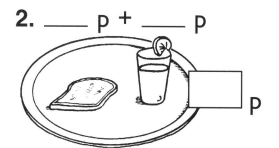

___ p

3. ___ p + ___ p

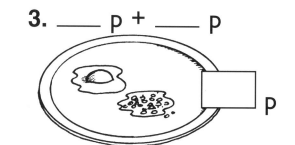

___ p

4. ___ p + ___ p

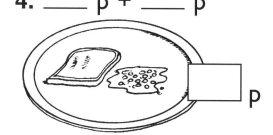

___ p

5. ___ p + ___ p

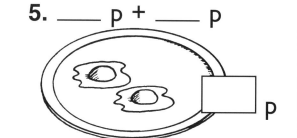

___ p

6. ___ p + ___ p

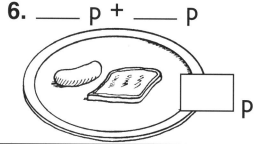

___ p

7. ___ p + ___ p

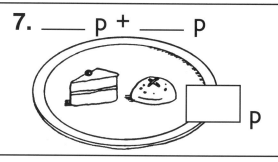

___ p

• Draw food to match the cost.

Now try this!

You can choose more than two items.

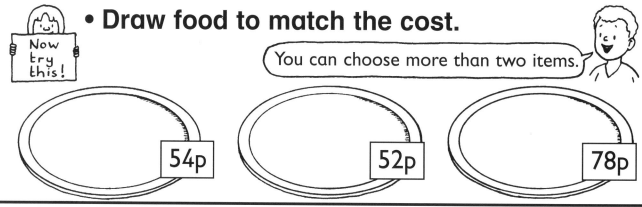

54p 52p 78p

Teachers' note This activity involves adding two-digit numbers without bridging. Use number grids or number tracks as appropriate (see pages 62 and 63), but encourage mental strategies if at all possible. It is important that children can partition numbers, add the parts and then recombine in order to carry out these calculations effectively.

Developing Numeracy Calculations Year 2 © A & C Black 2002

Give the dog a bone

- **Double** each number. Write on the bones.

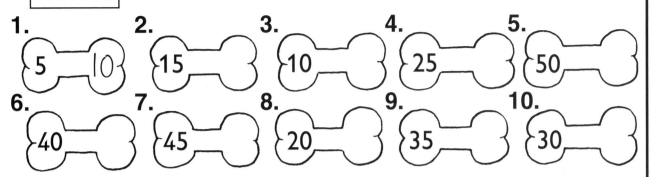

1. 5 10
2. 15
3. 10
4. 25
5. 50
6. 40
7. 45
8. 20
9. 35
10. 30

- **Follow your answers through the maze, in order. Draw the path from the dog to the bone.**

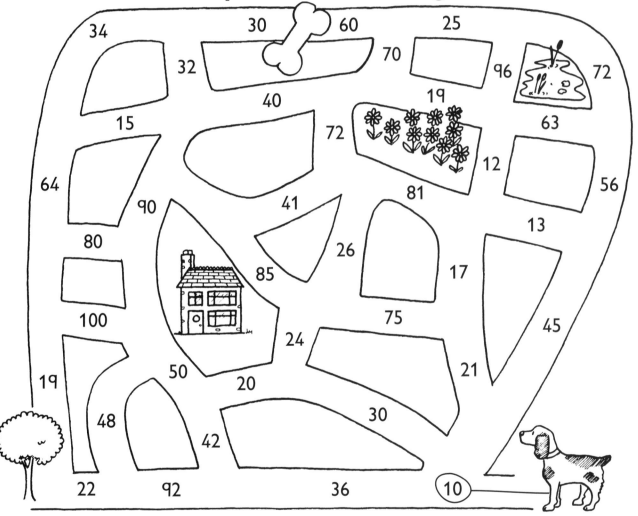

34   30   60   25
32   70   96   72
40   19   63
15   72   12   56
64   90   81   13
80   41   26   17
100   85   75   45
50   24   21
19   20   30
48   42
22   92   36   10

- **Find a route from the bone to the tree.**
- **Write** doubles clues **for the journey.**

Now try this!

Teachers' note The first activity involves doubling multiples of 5 up to 50. In the extension, some children could be challenged to use clues involving 'near doubles'.

Developing Numeracy
Calculations Year 2
© A & C Black 2002

Jack-in-a-box additions

To add 9, you can add 10, then take away 1.

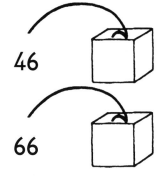

45 + 9 = 54

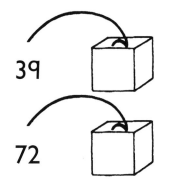

add 10

take away 1

40   50   60

• **Add 9 to these numbers.**

24 → 33   46 →   39 →

57 →   66 →   72 →

To add 11, first add 10, then add 1.

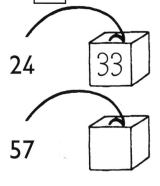

45 + 11 = 56

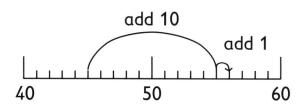

add 10

add 1

40   50   60

• **Add 11 to these numbers.**

24 →   28 →   49 →

56 →   74 →   89 →

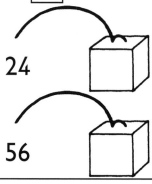

• **Choose your own numbers.**

• **Add 19.**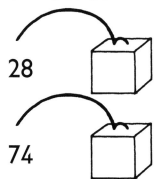

• **Add 21.**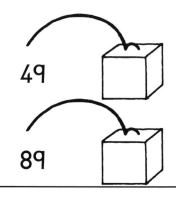

Teachers' note Give children plenty of practice in adding multiples of 10 to a range of two-digit numbers. Encourage mental methods, but if necessary use number grids or number tracks (see pages 62 and 63). Then discuss adding near multiples of 10 to two-digit numbers.

Developing Numeracy Calculations Year 2 © A & C Black 2002

Money boxes

• Write the ☐ total for each money box.

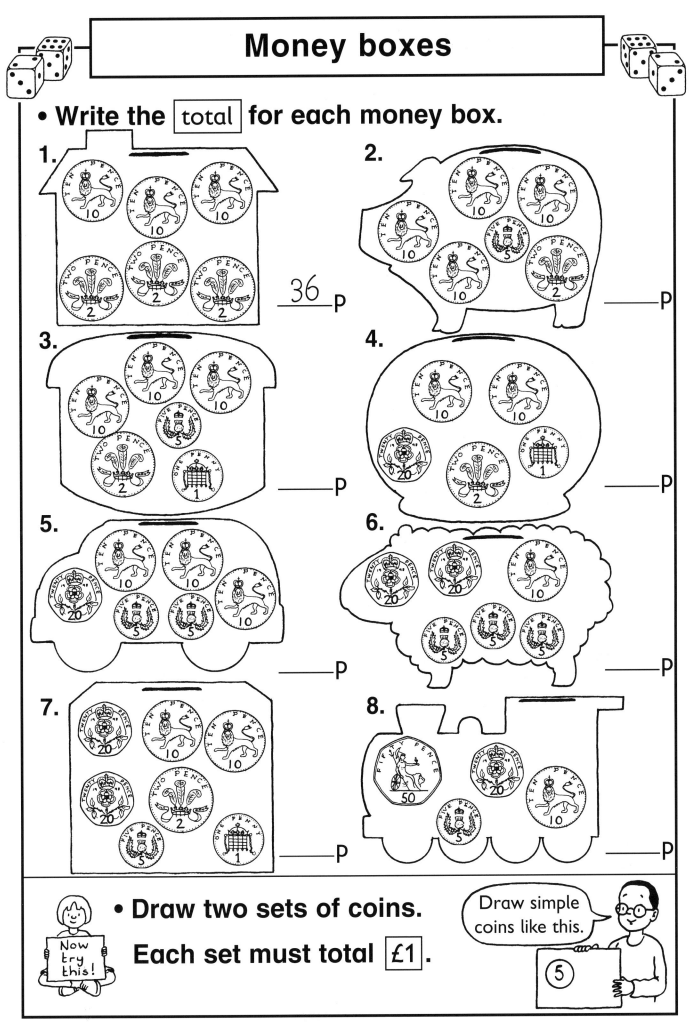

1. _____ 36 P

2. _____ P

3. _____ P

4. _____ P

5. _____ P

6. _____ P

7. _____ P

8. _____ P

• Draw two sets of coins.

Each set must total £1.

Draw simple coins like this.

⑤

Now try this!

Teachers' note Encourage the children to use mental strategies and to manage without number lines if possible. Discuss the strategies that they use. It will be helpful for children to start with the largest coins first. Some children may need real coins as an aid.

Developing Numeracy
Calculations Year 2
© A & C Black 2002

Sunglasses

- **Fill in the missing numbers.**

Each side must have the same answer.

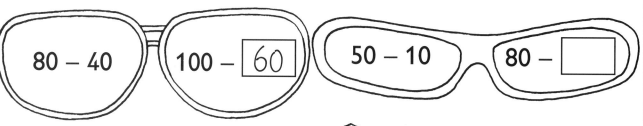

80 – 40   100 – [60]   50 – 10   80 – [ ]

100 – 70   40 – [ ]   90 – 50   70 – [ ]

80 – 50   [ ] – 10   70 – 20   [ ] – 30

60 – 50   [ ] – 70   80 – 30   [ ] – 50

400 – 100   600 – [ ]   900 – 300   700 – [ ]

- **Write your own subtractions.**

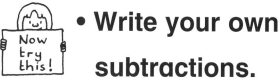

Each side must have the same answer.

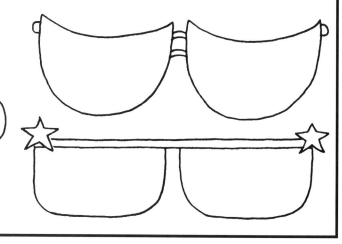

Teachers' note Children should be comfortable with subtracting multiples of 10 and 100. Encourage them to use known facts, for example, 8 – 4 = 4 can help them work out that 80 – 40 = 40. For the extension, you can either restrict the numbers to be used (for example, multiples of 10 or multiples of 100), or leave it open.

Developing Numeracy Calculations Year 2 © A & C Black 2002

- **Answer the subtractions.**
- **Use the code to change the answers into letters.**

a	b	c	d	e	f	g	h	i	j	k	l	m
21	22	23	24	25	26	27	28	29	30	31	32	33
n	o	p	q	r	s	t	u	v	w	x	y	z
34	35	36	37	38	39	40	41	42	43	44	45	46

$61 - 20 = 41$ u

$54 - 20 =$

$74 - 50 =$

$95 - 70 =$

$78 - 40 =$

$80 - 40 =$

$88 - 60 =$

$55 - 30 =$

$42 - 20 =$

$81 - 60 =$

$70 - 30 =$

$68 - 40 =$

$100 - 60 =$

$51 - 10 =$

$92 - 70 =$

Found it!

- **Where is the spider?** _____

Now try this!

- **Use the code to write your own message.**
- **Give it to a partner to solve.**

Teachers' note This activity involves subtracting a multiple of 10 from a two-digit number. The children could use a number grid if necessary (see page 62). However, encourage them to use mental strategies.

**Developing Numeracy
Calculations Year 2
© A & C Black 2002**

Big Ted, Little Ted

• **Find the** $\boxed{\text{difference}}$ **in height.**

1.

67 cm − 23 cm = $\boxed{44}$ cm

2.

65 cm − 44 cm = $\boxed{}$ cm

3.

48 cm − 36 cm = $\boxed{}$ cm

4.

96 cm − 74 cm = $\boxed{}$ cm

5.

72 cm − 51 cm = $\boxed{}$ cm

6.

77 cm − 44 cm = $\boxed{}$ cm

The difference in height is $\boxed{35 \text{ cm}}$ **.**

• **Write the height of the smaller teddy.**

58 cm $\boxed{}$ cm   76 cm $\boxed{}$ cm   99 cm $\boxed{}$ cm

---

Teachers' note This activity involves subtracting two-digit numbers without bridging. It is important that children can partition numbers, subtract the parts and then recombine in order to carry out these calculations effectively.

**Developing Numeracy
Calculations Year 2
© A & C Black 2002**

Close differences

- **Ring** | touching numbers | **that have a** | difference of 3 |.

- **Write how many pairs you find.** _____

Some pairs are **vertical**.

⟨41	38⟩	75	88	91	74
69	70	72	28	26	77
72	55	61	58	90	92
87	90	68	65	82	95

- **Write the missing numbers.**

26 + ☐ = 32   46 + ☐ = 51   72 + ☐ = 78

67 + ☐ = 76   39 + ☐ = 47   28 + ☐ = 35

72 − 68 = ☐   55 − 49 = ☐   91 − 87 = ☐

84 − 79 = ☐   41 − 35 = ☐   63 − 54 = ☐

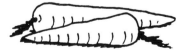

- **Write the missing numbers.**

Now try this!

95 + ☐ = 101   99 + ☐ = 105   97 + ☐ = 109

Teachers' note This activity involves finding the difference between a pair of close two-digit numbers. Explain that the most efficient way to find close differences is to count on from the smaller number to the larger. Encourage children to use this method, using number bonds to bridge over the multiple of ten.

Developing Numeracy Calculations Year 2 © A & C Black 2002

Jack-in-a-box subtractions

To subtract 9, take away 10, then add 1.

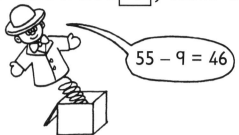

55 – 9 = 46

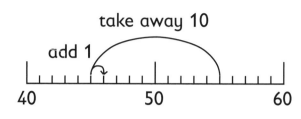

add 1 — take away 10

40   50   60

• **Subtract 9 from these numbers.**

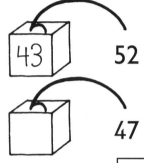 43   52

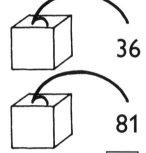 36

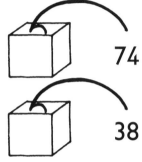 74

47   81   38

To subtract 11, take away 10, then take away 1.

55 – 11 = 44

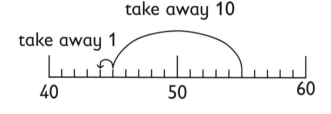

take away 1 — take away 10

40   50   60

• **Subtract 11 from these numbers.**

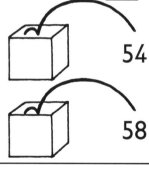 54

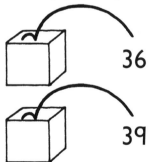 36

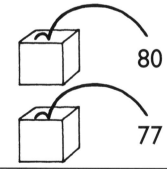 80

58   39   77

• **Choose your own numbers.**

• **Subtract 19.**   • **Subtract 21.**

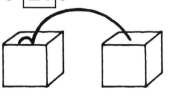

Teachers' note Give children plenty of practice in subtracting multiples of 10 from a range of two-digit numbers. Then discuss subtracting near multiples of 10 from two-digit numbers.

**Developing Numeracy
Calculations Year 2
© A & C Black 2002**

Bring and buy

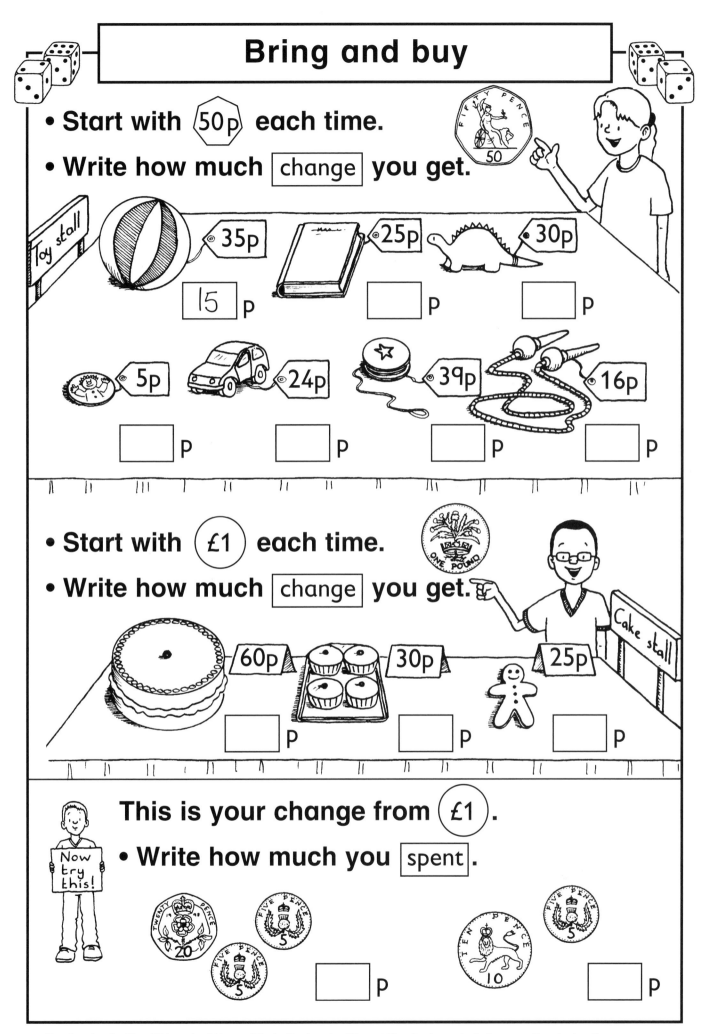

- **Start with** 50p **each time.**
- **Write how much** change **you get.**

Toy stall

35p → 15 P

25p → ☐ P

30p → ☐ P

5p → ☐ P

24p → ☐ P

39p → ☐ P

16p → ☐ P

- **Start with** £1 **each time.**
- **Write how much** change **you get.**

Cake stall

60p → ☐ P

30p → ☐ P

25p → ☐ P

This is your change from £1.

- **Write how much you** spent.

Now try this!

☐ P

☐ P

Teachers' note The children should be confident with changing 50p and £1 coins for equivalent amounts.

Developing Numeracy Calculations Year 2 © A & C Black 2002

Jumbo wordsearch

- **Write the answers.**

Answers can be **horizontal** or **vertical**.

- **Find and ring the number words.**

35 – 25 = | 10 | 25 + 25 = | | 74 – 14 = | |

28 + 12 = | | 92 – 22 = | | 15 + 15 = | |

95 – 15 = | | 45 + 45 = | | 38 – 18 = | |

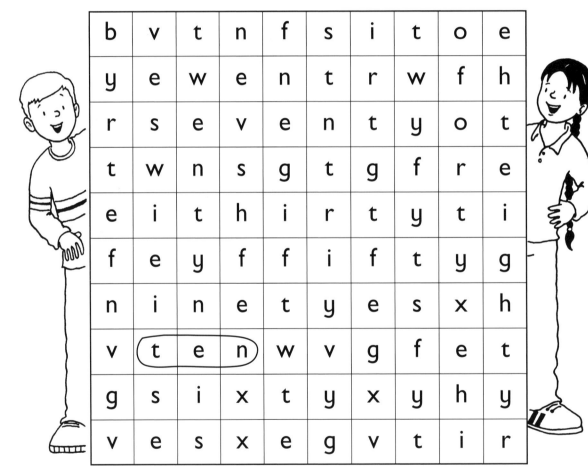

b	v	t	n	f	s	i	t	o	e
y	e	w	e	n	t	r	w	f	h
r	s	e	v	e	n	t	y	o	t
t	w	n	s	g	t	g	f	r	e
e	i	t	h	i	r	t	y	t	i
f	e	y	f	f	i	f	t	y	g
n	i	n	e	t	y	e	s	x	h
v	t	e	n	w	v	g	f	e	t
g	s	i	x	t	y	x	y	h	y
v	e	s	x	e	g	v	t	i	r

- **Write a new clue for each number you found in the wordsearch.**

Teachers' note This activity involves finding answers which are multiples of 10. Talk about an addition undoing a subtraction, and vice versa. Some children may need a word-bank to refer to.

Developing Numeracy Calculations Year 2 © A & C Black 2002

Twos

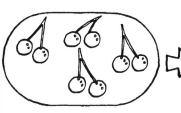

Multiplication is a quick way to add the same number lots of times.

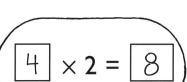

The sign we use is ×

• Write the missing numbers.

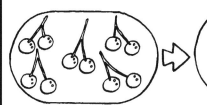 ⇨ 2 + 2 + 2 + 2
[4] groups of 2 ⇨ [4] × 2 = [8]

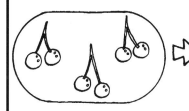 ⇨ 2 + 2 + 2 + 2 + 2
[ ] groups of [ ] ⇨ [ ] × 2 = [ ]

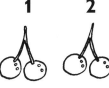 ⇨ [ ] + [ ] + [ ]
[ ] groups of [ ] ⇨ [ ] × [ ] = [ ]

• Write the answers to these multiplications.

1	2	3	4	5	6	7	8	9	10

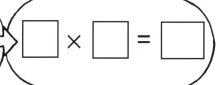

1 × 2 = [ ]   7 × 2 = [ ]   5 × 2 = [ ]

9 × 2 = [ ]   6 × 2 = [ ]   8 × 2 = [ ]

10 × 2 = [ ]   4 × 2 = [ ]   2 × 2 = [ ]

 Now try this! **• Write the missing numbers.**

[ ] × 2 = 10   [ ] × 2 = 16   [ ] × 2 = 18

Teachers' note Emphasise to the children that the order of multiplication does not matter, for example 4 x 2 = 2 x 4 (see also the note on multiplication on page 5). Children should know by heart the result of multiplying by 2 for numbers up to 10.

**Developing Numeracy
Calculations Year 2**
© A & C Black 2002

Fives

• **Write the missing numbers.**

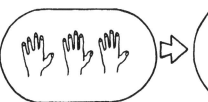 ⇨ 5 + 5 / [2] groups of 5 ⇨ [2] × 5 = [10]

(hands) ⇨ 5 + 5 + 5 + 5 / [ ] groups of [ ] ⇨ [ ] × 5 = [ ]

(hands) ⇨ [ ] + [ ] + [ ] / [ ] groups of [ ] ⇨ [ ] × [ ] = [ ]

• **Write the answers to these** multiplications **.**

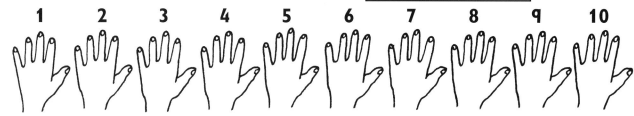

1   2   3   4   5   6   7   8   9   10

$1 \times 5 =$ [ ] $5 \times 5 =$ [ ] $7 \times 5 =$ [ ]

$9 \times 5 =$ [ ] $3 \times 5 =$ [ ] $6 \times 5 =$ [ ]

$4 \times 5 =$ [ ] $8 \times 5 =$ [ ] $10 \times 5 =$ [ ]

 • **Write the missing numbers.**

[ ] $\times 5 = 35$ [ ] $\times 5 = 45$ [ ] $\times 5 = 25$

[ ] $\times 5 = 40$ [ ] $\times 5 = 50$ [ ] $\times 5 = 30$

Teachers' note Emphasise to the children that the order of multiplication does not matter, for example 2 x 5 = 5 x 2 (see also the note on multiplication on page 5). Children should know by heart the result of multiplying by 5 for numbers up to 10.

**Developing Numeracy
Calculations Year 2
© A & C Black 2002**

46

Tens

- ## Write the missing numbers.

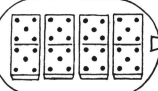 → $10 + 10 + 10 + 10$ [4] groups of 10 → [4] × 10 = [40]

 → $10 + 10$ [ ] groups of [ ] → [ ] × 10 = [ ]

 → [ ] + [ ] + [ ] [ ] groups of [ ] → [ ] × [ ] = [ ]

- ## Write the answers to these multiplications.

| 1 | 2 | 3 | 4 | 5 | 6 | 7 | 8 | 9 | 10 |

$1 \times 10 =$ [ ] $7 \times 10 =$ [ ] $5 \times 10 =$ [ ]

$9 \times 10 =$ [ ] $6 \times 10 =$ [ ] $2 \times 10 =$ [ ]

$4 \times 10 =$ [ ] $8 \times 10 =$ [ ] $10 \times 10 =$ [ ]

 Now try this!

- ## Write the missing numbers.

[ ] $\times 10 = 60$ [ ] $\times 10 = 90$ [ ] $\times 10 = 30$

[ ] $\times 10 = 80$ [ ] $\times 10 = 50$ [ ] $\times 10 = 100$

Teachers' note Emphasise to the children that the order of multiplication does not matter, for example 4 x 10 = 10 x 4 (see also the note on multiplication on page 5). Children should know by heart the result of multiplying by 10 for numbers up to 10.

Developing Numeracy Calculations Year 2 © A & C Black 2002

There are two ways you can write this pattern as a multiplication.

$5 \times 2 = 10$

$2 \times 5 = 10$

• **Write multiplication facts for each flowerbed.**

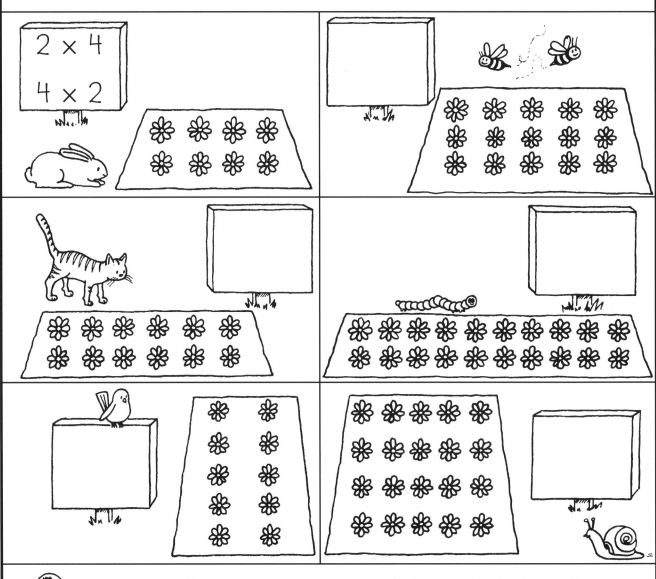

2×4

4×2

• **Draw flowers to show this multiplication.**

Now try this!

8×2

2×8

Teachers' note These array patterns are extremely useful for showing that the order of multiplication does not matter, for example showing that 2 x 5 = 5 x 2. Talk about square arrays such as 2 x 2, 3 x 3, 4 x 4 and 5 x 5. The children should know all multiplication facts which generate answers of 25 and below.

**Developing Numeracy
Calculations Year 2
© A & C Black 2002**

In the garden

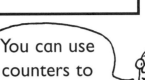

- **Write the missing numbers.**

You can use counters to help you.

$4 \times 2 = \boxed{}$ $3 \times 5 = \boxed{}$ $10 \times 6 = \boxed{}$

$5 \times 10 = \boxed{}$ $7 \times 2 = \boxed{}$ $5 \times 5 = \boxed{}$

$6 \times \boxed{} = 12$ $7 \times \boxed{} = 70$ $10 \times \boxed{} = 100$

$8 \times \boxed{} = 16$ $9 \times \boxed{} = 45$ $10 \times \boxed{} = 50$

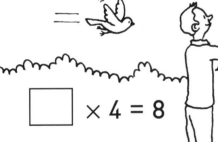

$\boxed{} \times 4 = 8$ $\boxed{} \times 6 = 12$ $\boxed{} \times 3 = 15$

$\boxed{} \times 5 = 25$ $\boxed{} \times 6 = 60$ $\boxed{} \times 7 = 14$

Now try this!

- **Complete the multiplication table .**

×	0	1	2	3	4	5	6	7	8	9	10
2	0	2	4	6							
5											
10											

Teachers' note Discuss the fact that the order of multiplication does not matter, for example 2 x 5 = 5 x 2. For the extension activity, check that the children know how to write a simple multiplication table.

**Developing Numeracy
Calculations Year 2
© A & C Black 2002**

Guinea pig shuffle

• Play this game with a partner.

☆ Cut out the guinea pig cards and the hutches.

☆ Shuffle the guinea pig cards. Spread them face down.

☆ Take turns to pick a card. Place it in the correct hutch.

☆ If it has no hutch, keep it.

☆ The winner is the player with the fewest cards at the end.

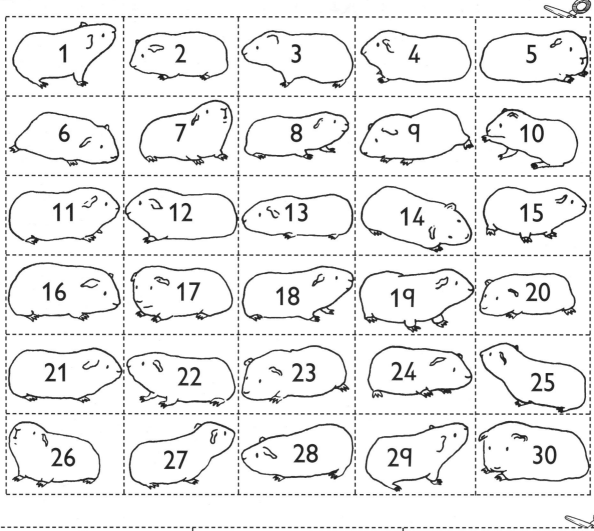

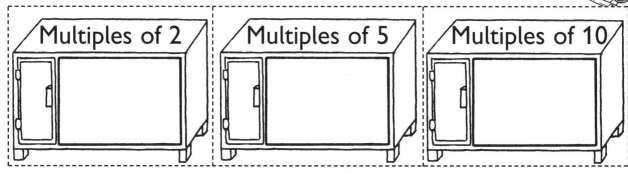

Multiples of 2   Multiples of 5   Multiples of 10

Teachers' note Before beginning the activity, talk about multiples and what the word means. Discuss that a number may be a multiple of more than one number. Provide counting aids if necessary, for example number lines or number tracks (see pages 62 and 63).

**Developing Numeracy
Calculations Year 2
© A & C Black 2002**

Sandcastles

- **Work out the multiplications.**

- **Write the answers on the sandcastles.**

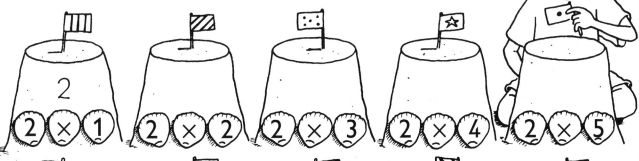

2

2×1 2×2 2×3 2×4 2×5

3×1 3×2 3×3 3×4 3×5

4×1 4×2 4×3 4×4 4×5

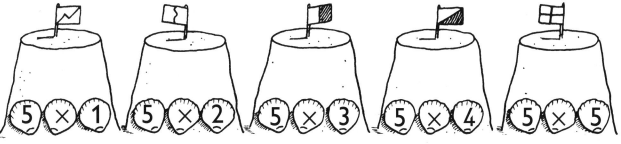

5×1 5×2 5×3 5×4 5×5

- **Write four different multiplications.**

Now try this!

☐ × ☐ = 12   ☐ × ☐ = 12

☐ × ☐ = 12   ☐ × ☐ = 12

Teachers' note This activity provides practice in multiplying a single digit up to 5 by 2, 3, 4 and 5. Provide counting aids if necessary, for example number lines or number tracks (see pages 62 and 63).

Developing Numeracy Calculations Year 2 © A & C Black 2002

Purses and keyrings

- Double each amount.

Doubling is the same as multiplying by 2.

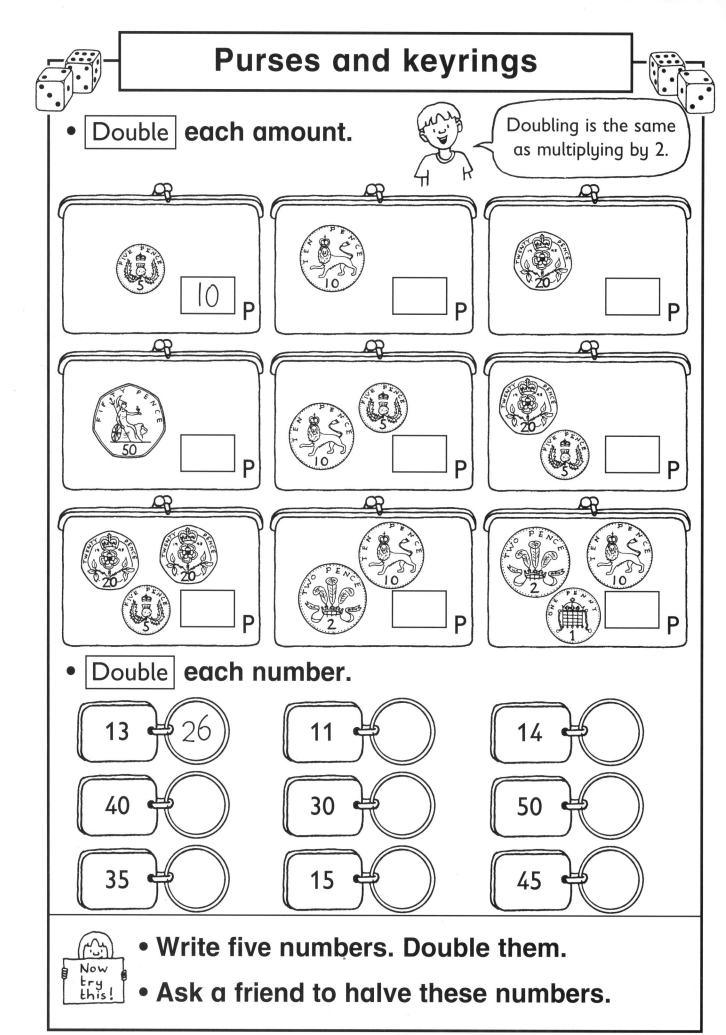

5 → **10** P	10 → ☐ P	20 → ☐ P
50 → ☐ P	10, 5 → ☐ P	20, 5 → ☐ P
20, 20, 5 → ☐ P	10, 2 → ☐ P	2, 10, 1 → ☐ P

- Double each number.

13 → 26	11 → ◯	14 → ◯
40 → ◯	30 → ◯	50 → ◯
35 → ◯	15 → ◯	45 → ◯

Now try this!

- **Write five numbers. Double them.**
- **Ask a friend to halve these numbers.**

Teachers' note Check that the children can double all numbers up to 15 and multiples of 5 up to 50. Provide counting aids if necessary, for example number lines or number tracks (see pages 62 and 63). For the extension, ensure the children understand that halving is the opposite of doubling.

Developing Numeracy Calculations Year 2 © A & C Black 2002

Equal shares

- **Share the treats** equally **between the dogs.**

1.

8 shared between 2 is 4

2.

☐ shared between 2 is ☐

3.

☐ shared between 2 is ☐

4.

☐ shared between 3 is ☐

5.

☐ shared between 3 is ☐

6.

☐ shared between 3 is ☐

You have 24 **treats.**

Use counters to help you.

24 shared between 2 is 12.

24 shared between 24 is 1.

- **Which other** equal shares **can you find?**

Now try this!

Teachers' note Children need to understand the difference between different types of division, for example, sharing between two and dividing into twos. The children can use various strategies, such as mental strategies, matching strategies and using counters. It is important that after answering each question, the children check they have shared the treats 'fairly'.

Developing Numeracy Calculations Year 2 © A & C Black 2002

53

Sharing sweets

- **Share the sweets** equally.
- **Find the** remainder.

The **remainder** is what is left over after sharing equally.

1.
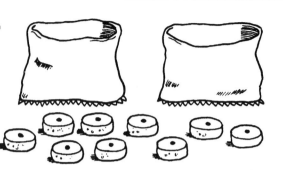

☐ shared between 2 is ☐

The remainder is ☐

2.

☐ shared between 3 is ☐

The remainder is ☐

3.

☐ shared between 3 is ☐

The remainder is ☐

4.

☐ shared between 4 is ☐

The remainder is ☐

- **Draw some sweets in the box.**
- **Complete the number sentence.**
- **Write the remainder.**

☐ shared between 4 is ☐

The remainder is ☐

Teachers' note Children need to understand the difference between different types of division, for example, sharing between two and dividing into twos. This activity looks at sharing with remainders. The children can use various strategies, such as mental strategies, matching strategies and using counters. Discuss the largest remainder possible when sharing between 2, 3, 4 and so on.

**Developing Numeracy
Calculations Year 2
© A & C Black 2002**

Grouping minibeasts

- **Complete each number sentence.**

- **Draw rings to show the groups.**

There are $\boxed{6}$ twos in 12.

There are $\boxed{}$ twos in 10.

There are $\boxed{}$ threes in 15.

There are $\boxed{}$ threes in 18.

There are $\boxed{}$ fours in 16.

 • **Complete these number sentences.**

There are $\boxed{}$ fours in 12.

There are $\boxed{}$ twos in 14.

Draw pictures to help you.

Teachers' note Children need to understand the difference between different types of division, for example, sharing between two and dividing into twos. This activity looks at grouping without remainders. Check that children interpret the extension activity correctly.

Developing Numeracy Calculations Year 2 © A & C Black 2002

Dividing by 2

- $\boxed{\text{Divide}}$ **each number on the clown by** $\boxed{2}$ **.**

- **Use the code to colour the clown.**

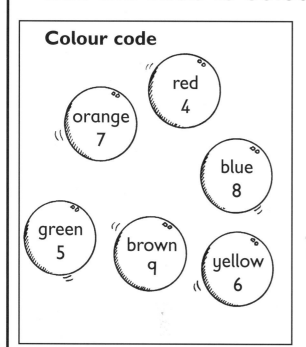

Colour code

red
4

orange
7

blue
8

green
5

brown
9

yellow
6

- **Answer each** $\boxed{\text{division}}$ **.**

$\div$ means **divide by.**

$8 \div 2 = \boxed{}$ $6 \div 2 = \boxed{}$ $4 \div 2 = \boxed{}$

$12 \div 2 = \boxed{}$ $16 \div 2 = \boxed{}$ $20 \div 2 = \boxed{}$

$18 \div 2 = \boxed{}$ $14 \div 2 = \boxed{}$ $10 \div 2 = \boxed{}$

- **Write the missing number.**

Divide 8 by 2 → $\boxed{}$

Share 16 between 2 → $\boxed{}$

How many twos in 18? → $\boxed{}$

What is 12 divided by 2? → $\boxed{}$

Teachers' note Decide what aids, if any, are needed to support the children. Some children will benefit from using counters, others could be encouraged to write out the two times table facts and use these to answer the divisions. Discuss the link between division facts and multiplication facts, for example, if 4 x 2 = 8, then 8 ÷ 2 = 4.

**Developing Numeracy
Calculations Year 2
© A & C Black 2002**

Dividing by 5

- **Divide** each number on the clown by **5**.

- **Use the code to colour the clown.**

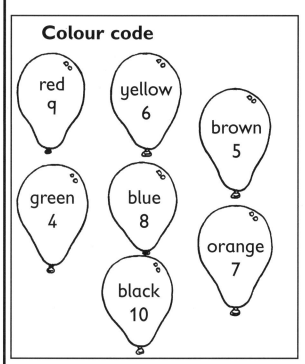

Colour code

red 9

yellow 6

brown 5

green 4

blue 8

orange 7

black 10

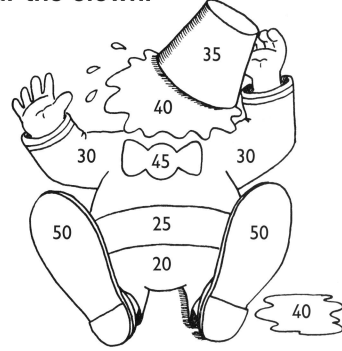

- **Answer each** division.

Remember, ÷ means **divide by.**

$10 \div 5 = \boxed{}$ $30 \div 5 = \boxed{}$ $40 \div 5 = \boxed{}$

$20 \div 5 = \boxed{}$ $25 \div 5 = \boxed{}$ $50 \div 5 = \boxed{}$

$15 \div 5 = \boxed{}$ $35 \div 5 = \boxed{}$ $45 \div 5 = \boxed{}$

Now try this!

- **Fill in the missing number.**

Divide 35 by 5 → $\boxed{}$

Share 50 between 5 → $\boxed{}$

How many fives in 45? → $\boxed{}$

What is 30 divided by 5? → $\boxed{}$

Teachers' note Decide what aids, if any, are needed to support the children. Some children will benefit from using counters, others could be encouraged to write out the five times table facts and use these to answer the divisions. Discuss the link between division facts and multiplication facts, for example, if 4 x 5 = 20, then 20 ÷ 5 = 4.

**Developing Numeracy
Calculations Year 2
© A & C Black 2002**

Dividing by 10

- **Join each mole to the correct mole hill.**

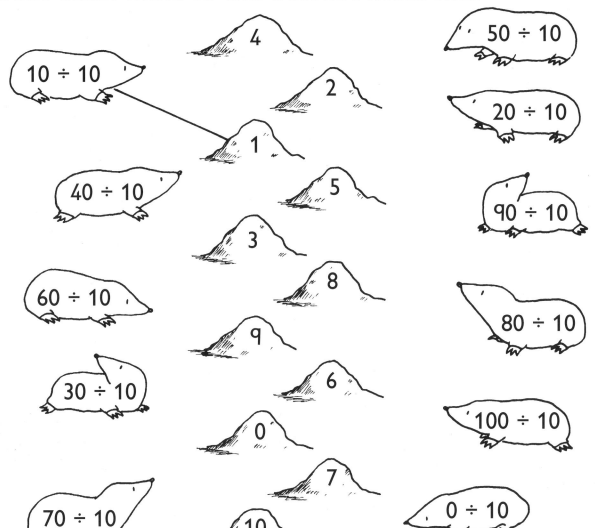

- **Use the code to change the answers into letters.**

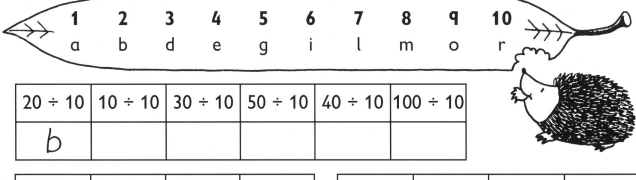

1	2	3	4	5	6	7	8	9	10
a	b	d	e	g	i	l	m	o	r

20 ÷ 10	10 ÷ 10	30 ÷ 10	50 ÷ 10	40 ÷ 10	100 ÷ 10
b					

80 ÷ 10	90 ÷ 10	70 ÷ 10	40 ÷ 10		20 ÷ 10	60 ÷ 10	100 ÷ 10	30 ÷ 10

Teachers' note Decide what aids, if any, are needed to support the children. Some children will benefit from using a number grid or number track (see pages 62 and 63), others could be encouraged to write out the ten times table facts and use these to answer the divisions. Discuss the link between division facts and multiplication facts, for example, if 4 x 10 = 40, then 40 ÷ 10 = 4.

**Developing Numeracy
Calculations Year 2
© A & C Black 2002**

The tortoise and the hare

• Answer the divisions.

start 	16 ÷ 2 [8]	70 ÷ 10 [ ]	60 ÷ 10 [ ]	14 ÷ 2 [ ]	4 ÷ 2 [ ]	
	10 ÷ 10 [ ]	50 ÷ 5 [ ]	90 ÷ 10 [ ]	25 ÷ 5 [ ]	80 ÷ 10 [ ]	finish
start	18 ÷ 2 [ ]	16 ÷ 1 [ ]	20 ÷ 5 [ ]	8 ÷ 2 [ ]	15 ÷ 5 [ ]	

My answers equal **9 or more**. Colour them red.

My answers equal **5, 6, 7** or **8**. Colour them blue.

• Who reaches the finish? _____

The answers are in the centre.

• Write the missing numbers.

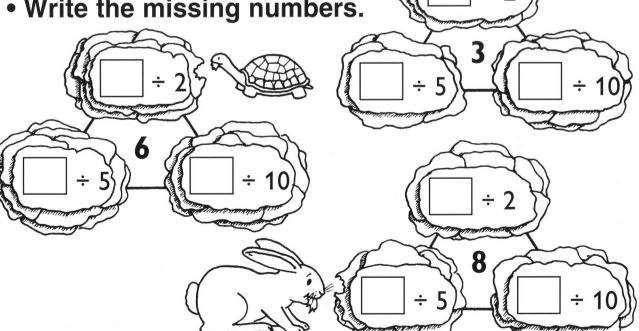

Teachers' note Discuss with the children what aids, if any, they think they might need to solve the problems.

**Developing Numeracy
Calculations Year 2
© A & C Black 2002**

Money boxes and keys

- **Halve** **each amount.**

 Halving is the same as dividing by 2.

 **5** P

 P

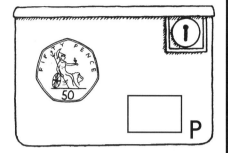 P

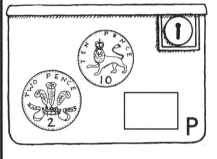 P

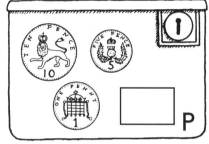 P

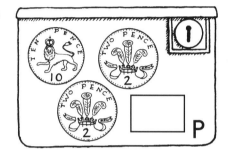 P

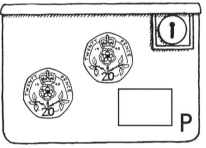 P

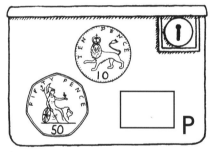 P

 P

- **Halve** **each number.**

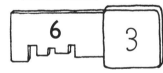 6 — 3

26 —

22 —

28 —

80 —

10 —

70 —

30 —

90 —

 Now try this!

- **Write five** **even** **numbers. Halve them.**
- **Ask a friend to double these numbers.**

Teachers' note Check that the children can halve all numbers up to 30 and multiples of 10 up to 100. Provide counting aids if necessary, for example number lines or number tracks (see pages 62 and 63). Ensure the children understand that halving is the opposite of doubling.

Developing Numeracy
Calculations Year 2
© A & C Black 2002

Tug of war

- ## Answer the calculation on each child.

- ## Find the total for each team.

The largest total wins.

3 × 2	6 × 5	50 ÷ 10	30 ÷ 5
6			

10 × 3	2 × 2	35 ÷ 5	14 ÷ 2

Total = _____   Total = _____

9 × 5	2 × 7	30 ÷ 10	16 ÷ 2

5 × 7	6 × 2	45 ÷ 5	18 ÷ 2

Total = _____   Total = _____

Now try this!

- ## Look at this scarf.

The first number in each calculation is the answer to the calculation before it.

20 ÷ 2	10 + 6	16 ÷ 2	8 − 4	4 × 10	40 − 30	10 × 2

- ## Make up your own scarf.

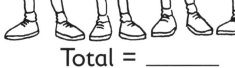

Teachers' note For the extension activity, suggest that the last answer should equal the first number on the scarf. Encourage the children to use all four operations.

Developing Numeracy Calculations Year 2 © A & C Black 2002

Number grid

0	1	2	3	4	5	6	7	8	9
10	11	12	13	14	15	16	17	18	19
20	21	22	23	24	25	26	27	28	29
30	31	32	33	34	35	36	37	38	39
40	41	42	43	44	45	46	47	48	49
50	51	52	53	54	55	56	57	58	59
60	61	62	63	64	65	66	67	68	69
70	71	72	73	74	75	76	77	78	79
80	81	82	83	84	85	86	87	88	89
90	91	92	93	94	95	96	97	98	99
100									

Developing Numeracy
Calculations Year 2
© A & C Black 2002

Number track

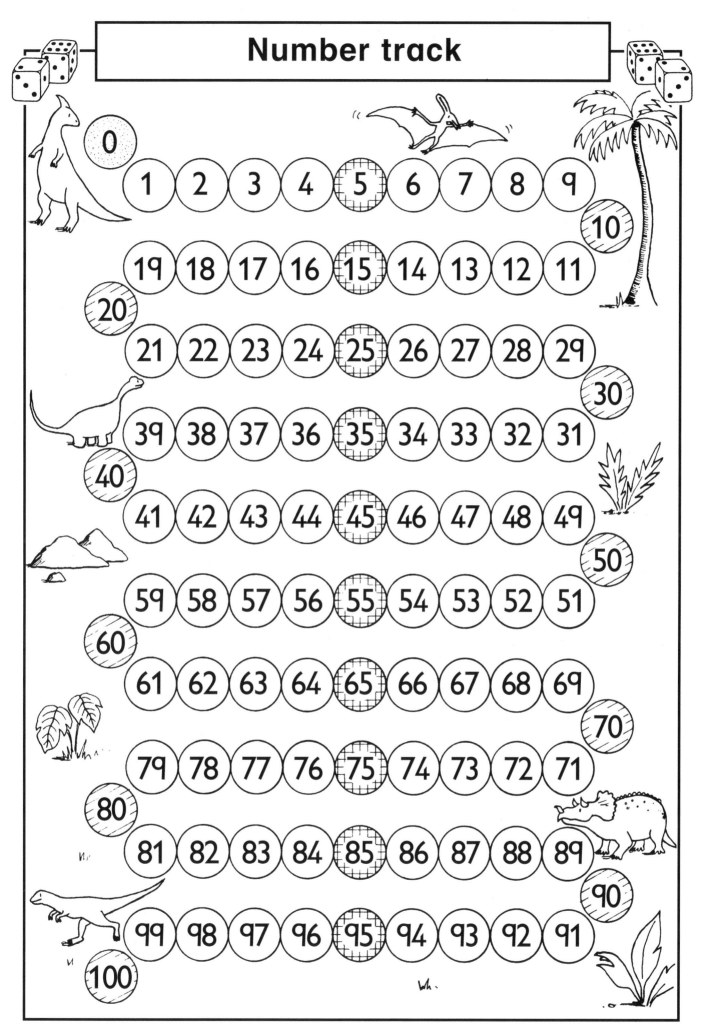

Developing Numeracy
Calculations Year 2
© A & C Black 2002

Answers

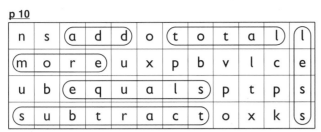

p 10

n	s	a	d	d	o	t	o	t	a	l	l
m	o	r	e	u	x	p	b	v	l	c	e
u	b	e	q	u	a	l	s	p	t	p	s
s	u	b	t	r	a	c	t	o	x	k	s

t	w	e	l	v	e	a	f	j	k	h	g
l	p	q	o	u	f	o	u	r	o	n	e
v	e	i	g	h	t	t	s	e	s	k	t
n	b	j	y	m	h	x	e	r	s	t	h
i	a	e	t	e	n	l	v	z	i	w	r
n	f	i	v	e	w	g	e	c	x	o	e
e	e	l	e	v	e	n	n	d	d	e	e

Now try this!
eleven

p 14
The mystery words are 'square' and 'circle'.

p 19
Frog 8 has no log. Check children's own calculations.

p 21
The missing numbers are 8, 13 and 16. Check children's own calculations.

p 22

+	4	7	9
6	10	13	15
5	9	12	14
8	12	15	17

+	5	6	8
4	9	10	12
7	12	13	15
9	14	15	17

+	7	3	9
4	11	7	13
8	15	11	17
9	16	12	18

4	+	8	=	12
+		+		+
6	+	1	=	7
=		=		=
10	+	9	=	19

Now try this!

8	+	2	+	1	=	11
–		+		+		–
7	+	3	–	2	=	8
+		+		+		+
4	+	2	–	2	=	4
=		=		=		=
5	+	7	–	5	=	7

p 28
The trail leads to the frog.

p 32

p 34
1. 21p + 11p = 32p
2. 20p + 15p = 35p
3. 24p + 23p = 47p
4. 20p + 23p = 43p
5. 24p + 24p = 48p
6. 30p + 20p = 50p
7. 18p + 21p = 39p

Now try this!
Answer include:
54p – sausage and egg **or** chips and beans
52p – sausage and biscuit **or** bun and chips
78p – beans, egg and chips **or** two eggs and a sausage

p 39
The code words read 'under the bath tub'.

p 41   There are nine pairs:

41	38	75	88	91	74
69	70	72	28	26	77
72	55	61	58	90	92
87	90	68	65	82	95

p 44

b	v	t	n	f	s	i	t	o	e
y	e	w	e	n	t	r	w	f	h
r	s	e	v	e	n	t	y	o	t
t	w	n	s	g	t	g	f	r	e
e	i	t	h	i	r	t	y	t	i
f	e	y	f	f	i	f	t	y	g
n	i	n	e	t	y	e	s	x	h
v	t	e	n	w	v	g	f	e	t
g	s	i	x	t	y	x	y	h	y
v	e	s	x	e	g	v	t	i	r

p 58
The code words are 'badger', 'mole' and 'bird'.

p 59
The tortoise reaches the finish.

p 61
The totals are: 47, 48, 70 and 65.